W9-CFC-149

COLLEGE BOUND

How to Prepare, Pick, & Pay Less for College in the 21st Century

JASON FRANKLIN

© 2013 Learn To Perform, LLC
All Rights Reserved.

No part of this publication may be reproduced, stored in a retrieval system, or transmitted, in
any form or by any means, electronic, mechanical, photocopying, recording, or otherwise,
without the written permission of the author.

First published by Dog Ear Publishing
4010 W. 86th Street, Ste H
Indianapolis, IN 46268
www.dogearpublishing.net

ISBN: 978-1-4575-2606-0
Library of Congress Control Number: *applied for*

This book is printed on acid free paper.
Printed in the United States of America

Table of Contents

I would like to thank my parents who made me pay for my own college, because they taught me that I would have a greater appreciation for my education if it was funded by my hard earned money. They were right.

I would like to thank my wife and kids who were very patient with me as I spent many months working on this project. I love you all.

I would like to thank Annie Luhrsen who edited this book numerous times, provided suggestions, offered invaluable feedback as well as constantly encouraged me throughout the entire process. I could not ask for a better associate.

Finally, I would like to thank the thousands of families who I have had the privilege of serving over the years. Your feedback and willingness to share your experiences with me has been invaluable.

"And whatsoever ye do in word or deed, do all in the name of the Lord Jesus, giving thanks to God and the Father by him."
Colossians 3.17

Chapter 1

Why this book?

I have had, and continue to have, the privilege of working with some of the top college-bound high school students throughout Central Illinois as well as their very proactive parents. The ages of the students I work with stays the same every year while the world continues to change dramatically.

I have personally trained over 10,000 students for the ACT test. I hear their concerns and fears about college. They have good reason to be concerned. Consider the following statistics:

Since 1978 the cost of obtaining a college degree
has increased over 1,000%.

During that same time period medical expenses have gone up 601% and the price of food went up 244%.[1]

In 2012 there were over two million recent college graduates unemployed.[2]

In 1992, there were 5.1 million "underemployed" college graduates in the United States.

In 2008, there were 17.4 million "underemployed" college graduates in the United States.[3]

More than a third of recent college grads with jobs are working in positions that don't require a degree.[4]

Federal statistics reveal that only 36% of the full-time students who began college in 2001 received a bachelor's degree within four years.[5]

For the first time this century starting salaries for college graduates went down in 2008, then again 2009, and then again in 2010.[6]

THE MOST IMPORTANT FACT

According to a recent survey, a staggering 85% of college seniors planned to **move back home** after graduation in May.[7]

There is nothing wrong with a college graduate moving back home as long as the person has a job or is working to get full-time employment. My sister did this and saved thousands of dollars while working at State Farm National Headquarters in Bloomington, IL. A few years later, she got married and her savings were definitely a major asset when she and her husband began their new life.

I, on the other hand, had no intention of moving back home. I wanted to be independent and spent almost all my money learning how expensive life can be when you are not in the "protected" environment of college. My sister and I both went different routes, learned different lessons, experienced different outcomes, and are both content today. However, we went through college in a different time.

I went to high school in the 80s, graduated in the spring of 1990, and finished my college education in the early 90s. The economy was expanding. The internet was new. There were new markets and new job opportunities. The question was not whether or not I would get a job but rather which job and where. My siblings, who also attended college in the 90s, were in the same situation. Now, fast forward to the 21st Century.

The statistics on the previous page reveal a different world. A college degree does not necessarily guarantee employment. We hear on the national news that the unemployment rate is much lower for college graduates and that is certainly true. However, those numbers represent ALL college graduates regardless of age.

At the time of this writing I am 41 years old; I am included in those statistics as being employed. A recent college graduate is not going to be 41 years old with decades of work experience. That's why those statistics are important and parents need to keep them as a reminder to their high school students that college does not guarantee better employment. For emphasis, I will share three of those numbers again.

In 2012 there were over two million
recent college graduates unemployed.

In 1992, there were 5.1 million "underemployed"
college graduates in the United States.

In 2008, there were 17.4 million "underemployed"
college graduates in the United States.

I have six children and, at the time of this writing, my wife is pregnant
with our seventh child. I am not paying for their college. I am not
going to mislead them into thinking college automatically makes life
better, because it does not. Do I believe there is a value associated with
going to college and earning a degree? Absolutely. I also believe there
is a specific approach in guiding a student to understanding the process
of preparing, picking, and paying for college in a responsible manner.
Further, this approach will help prepare them for life after college. This
is why I have written this book.

NOTE: I share numerous of stories from past students and families throughout this book. Student names are changed in order to protect identity. I follow this policy in my ACT classes, seminars, and any materials associated with my work.

When appropriate I share information and stories about various colleges and universities. However, keep in mind that school policy and scholarship incentives can change from year to year. These true stories serve as illustrations, not guarantees that your student will get the very same scholarship at a particular school.

Many parents contact with me with great questions. Throughout the book you will see questions in bold followed by my response.

This book is written to parents with the understanding that their student will read it as well. However, there are sections where I specifically write to the students due to the nature of the material in that particular part.

IMPORTANT: All scholarships mentioned in this book are merit-based, not needs-based, scholarships unless otherwise noted.

Chapter 2

College Costs
The Rising Tide

College costs continue to dramatically increase every year regardless of national economic conditions. We are going to examine the cost increases during the first twelve complete academic school years in the 21st Century by reviewing them in two sets of six year periods. I selected schools that are located relatively close to my Central Illinois live ACT classes; however, the increases were seen throughout the country.

The Economy is Growing				
College/University	2000 – 01	2006 – 07	% increase	$ increase
Bradley University	$21,540	$28,200	31%	$6,660
Eastern Illinois University	$10,382	$14,819	43%	$4,437
Illinois College	$17,260	$24,000	39%	$6,740
Illinois State University	$11,558	$16,553	43%	$4,995
Illinois Wesleyan University	$26,860	$35,480	32%	$8,620
MacMurray College	$18,890	$22,839	21%	$3,949
Millikin University	$22,847	$29,805	31%	$6,958
Northern Illinois University	$9,301	$16,542	78%	$7,241
Northwestern University	$34,986	$45,163	29%	$10,177
Olivet Nazarene University	$19,424	$26,090	34%	$6,666
Southern Illinois University	$11,108	$15,628	41%	$4,520
University of Illinois (C-U)	$13,016	$19,240	48%	$6,224
Washington University	$35,070	$44,836	28%	$9,766
Western Illinois University	$11,595	$17,750	53%	$6,155

Source: U.S. Department of Education Institute of Education Sciences
http://nces.ed.gov/collegenavigator/

The above table begins with the school year after the Y2K scare. Most high school students were too young to remember the national media spending a lot of time building panic among the populace that the world will "shut down" on New Year's Day, 2000. It didn't happen. The following school year unfortunately began with 9/11: the most devastating terrorist attack on American soil in our nation's history. Our country was just coming out of a recession due to the Dot-Com Bubble Bust in the late 90s. Within hours of 9/11, our economy collapsed due to fear. However, the new War on Terror soon changed things.

War tends to make Americans patriotic. America united. Our foreign policy changed: we will not fight terrorism here, we will fight it abroad. Most Americans supported this change because they wanted to go on with their lives and raising their families. However, the economy was still slow due to 9/11 as the stock market bottomed out at 7,286 on October 7th, 2002.[8]

Soon every American received tax cuts. The economy responded. Unemployment dropped below 4 percent and remained there for many months. Home ownership was at all-time highs and property values soared. With the exception of events related to a few natural disasters, gas prices stayed for the most part below $2 per gallon through this six year period. The stock market took off, breaking the 14,000 mark in October of 2007.[9]

You may be asking, what does that have to do with college costs? Look at the table again. While the previously mentioned events were occurring, most were not paying attention to what colleges were doing in regard to pricing because in the 20th Century college costs were never really a concern.

There are colleges that have been around longer than we have been a country. Some of the Ivy League schools were founded in the late 1600s. During the previous centuries college costs did not go up that much. However, the economy was strong and families had more money. The increased cost of a college education really did not create a national buzz during that six year period shown in the previous table.

Anyone who has lived for an extended period of time can tell you that the economy works in cycles: it goes up and it goes down. Even though the economy was in a growth period, the housing market crash was coming. Examine the next table.

The Economy is Struggling				
College/University	2006 – 07	2012 – 13	% increase	$ increase
Bradley University	$28,200	$40,330	43%	$12,130
Eastern Illinois University	$14,819	$23,528	59%	$8,709
Illinois College	$24,000	$37,400	56%	$13,400
Illinois State University	$16,553	$25,416	54%	$8,863
Illinois Wesleyan University	$35,480	$48,522	37%	$13,042
MacMurray College	$22,839	$31,550	38%	$8,711
Millikin University	$29,805	$40,432	36%	$10,627
Northern Illinois University	$16,542	$28,000	69%	$11,458
Northwestern University	$45,163	$60,840	35%	$15,677
Olivet Nazarene University	$26,090	$39,690	52%	$13,600
Southern Illinois University	$15,628	$24,435	56%	$8,807
University of Illinois (C-U)	$19,240	28,564	49%	$9,324
Washington University	$44,836	$60,345	35%	$15,509
Western Illinois University	$17,750	$24,375	37%	$6,625

Source: U.S. Department of Education Institute of Education Sciences
http://nces.ed.gov/collegenavigator/

In the summer of 2008, everything seemed to fall apart quickly: General Motors, major banks, the housing crash, unemployment rose to over 10 percent, and the stock market crashed (eventually bottoming out at 6,507 on March 9th, 2009[10] – a far cry from 14,000).

Now, instead of families seeing their household income go up every year like it did during the previous six-year period, the opposite was happening. People were losing their jobs. Individuals were having their working hours reduced. Families were losing their homes. When this happens families begin budgeting every dollar, budget more carefully, and cut back on spending. Not colleges. They just kept on spending and raising their costs. Notice that 12 of the 14 schools listed in the tables increased their costs more during the bad economic times than during the economic growth period.

Now, we will put the information from the previous tables together and connect this specifically to college in the 21st Century.

So what happened in 12 years? Underestimated Four Year Costs				
College/University	2000 – 01	2012 – 13	% increase	$ increase
Bradley University	$86,160	$161,320	87%	$75,160
Eastern Illinois University	$41,528	$94,112	127%	$52,584
Illinois College	$69,040	$149,600	117%	$80,560
Illinois State University	$46,232	$101,664	120%	$55,432
Illinois Wesleyan University	$107,440	$194,088	81%	$86,648
MacMurray College	$75,560	$126,200	67%	$50,640
Millikin University	$91,388	$161,728	77%	$70,340
Northern Illinois University	$37,204	$112,000	201%	$74,796
Northwestern University	$139,944	$243,360	74%	$103,416
Olivet Nazarene University	$77,696	$158,760	104%	$81,064
Southern Illinois University	$44,432	$97,740	120%	$53,308
University of Illinois (C-U)	$52,064	$114,256	120%	$62,192
Washington University	$140,280	$241,380	72%	$101,100
Western Illinois University	$46,380	$97,500	110%	$51,120

Examine this table closely with your student, particularly the last column. These increases took place within a twelve year period: the same length of time your student will spend in the public education system. No financial planner could have predicted these dramatic increases. Families could not have known how much money they would need to set aside to cover the increases in the costs of college.

At the time of this writing, I have a son going into kindergarten. If we assume he is going to go to Northwestern University then that is going to cost him approximately a half million dollars. That sounds ridiculous and yet based on the above that's what happened during the first part of this century.

How will I pay for college?

I have six kids with a seventh on the way. My father paid for his college. I had to pay for my college which included leaving school twice, so I could work in order to pay for college. If every parent refused to pay for their kids' college education, then the costs of college would go dramatically down. It is your student's job to pay for college, so I encourage you to place the responsibility on them.

When I taught in the public schools, I had a student who was failing a required math class he needed to pass in order to graduate from high school. The kid was lazy and made no effort to do his homework. In a meeting, his dad shared that he told his son that if he just graduated from high school then the dad would pay for his entire college education. I could not believe it! Why make a deal with a student who could not survive high school and clearly was not motivated by the great incentive his dad had offered.

There are a great deal of parents who assume it is their responsibility to pay for college. I honestly believe over the years this has created a lot of peer pressure among parents creating this sense that parents are obligated to pay for college. Don't give in to this pressure. Any student can work a part-time job and pay for a quality two-year college education at a community college.

Will we be able to afford sending our student to the college of her choice?

If you can afford to help, then that is truly a gift and your student needs to understand that. When most students paid for their own college, or most of it, then college was affordable. As soon as the attitude changed to parents being expected to pay for the children's college education, then it made it much easier for universities to raise their costs. Ironically, the more parents got involved in financing college the lower four year college graduation rates sunk. (This is covered in a later section.)

If you were going to help your student purchase a car, would you start with a price range? If you family needed to move to another city and you need to find a home, would you start with a price range? For most, the answers would be of course. Then why do families view selecting a college differently?

Decide how much is realistic to contribute to your student's college education. Then help your student find a college that works financially. You will be teaching your student valuable financial lessons that will serve them well for years to come. We live in a country where our political leaders think nothing of debt. However, just look at what is happening in Europe. Debt is serious. Don't take it lightly and I encourage you not to start teaching your student that debt is okay by choosing a college that financially is not realistic.

For decades people were told that their home would be their greatest investment. However, the last five years have proven that a home can also be one's greatest liability. There are no guarantees when it comes to investments. College is no different. Be careful. Students, with the help of their parents, need to think beyond the college years. Minimize debt as much as possible.

Dave Ramsey is arguably one of the top financial coaches in the world. He has some very easy to read financial counseling books:

- The Total Money Makeover: A Proven Plan for Financial Fitness

- How to Have More than Enough: A Step-by-Step Guide to Creating Abundance

- Financial Peace Revisited

- EntreLeadership: 20 Years of Practical Business Wisdom from the Trenches

These would be ideal books for your student to read before going to college and, if possible, before looking at colleges. The last book would be a great source for students planning to major in business.

EMAIL: an exchange between Jason and a senior through the last stage of her college decision

Hi Jason,

This is Mindy, I took your class last spring and am now trying to make a college decision and am really torn. I thought you would have some good advice.

My last two schools that it comes down to are Texas Christian University and University of Kentucky.

I went to visit TCU in the fall and fell in love with it. It's a private school with some smaller classes but has the school spirit of a big school. The people were very warm, I loved the area of Fort Worth and the Texas culture, and its business program is pretty well respected. Tuition at TCU is $34,000, I got a scholarship for half tuition so we would pay $17,000 plus $10,000 for room and board, making the grand total $27,000 per year.

My parents will pay up to $18,000 per year, so I would have $9,000 in debt x 4 years = $36,000 in loans. That doesn't include the cost to study abroad or go on a trip with friends, etc. Also, a friend of mine goes there, and her mom told me that in order to afford the sorority she's in, Amanda has to put all of her money from her summer job (of working full time for more than minimum wage) towards the costs.

Seeing the debt I would have and hearing about my friend Amanda makes me a bit apprehensive about going to TCU, especially when I feel like it would be a wealthier group of kids down there. I get the sense that I would be one of the few who have loans. But I can't seem to forget how much I loved it and how I felt like I would fit right in when I visited. Oh, and when my dad asked about more money they said there was nothing they could do…Also, I am in the honors program at TCU.

My boyfriend goes to the University of Kentucky, so I didn't even consider it until after I visited this spring and saw my final price. I actually only applied there because he said I'd get a lot of scholarships, but wasn't too enthusiastic about it. I didn't want to follow him, and anyways, I was in love with TCU and sure I would go there until I heard about the prices of everything.

But I went to visit in February and definitely didn't fall in love with UK right away like I did at TCU. But I did like the campus a lot. Everything was very nice and I admired the school spirit they had. I am probably going to major in business and their business school has a program called Global Scholars where the students get their major, and by completing the program also get an international business minor (which is perfect for me because I wanted to also minor in Spanish.) The tuition at UK is $20,000 for out of state, and I got a $4,500 per year scholarship, which after adding room and board would be pretty close to the price of TCU so I told my parents we could just cross UK off the list.

But while we visited, my dad (**parents and Mindy attended Jason's family seminar**) talked to the financial aid office on my behalf, told them I'm a good student, and they said they would look for more money for me, and two weeks later, I got an extra $3,000. This would make tuition cost $12,500 per year, plus $10,000 for room and board (which is actually a high estimate) so the total would be about $23,000 a year, giving me $5,000 a year in debt x 4 which is $20,000 or even less since that was a high estimate for room and board and I am waiting to hear on a departmental scholarship.

I like Kentucky and know I would enjoy it and fit in there, and they're an all-around respected school, but I am already tired of hearing people mention that my boyfriend goes there so that's probably why I applied, etc. I know people will think I'm following him, which is the last thing I want. But the price seems less scary to me and it's a good school. Also, I'm wait listed for UK honors, but it is more likely I would get into

Global Scholars, and most people don't do both honors and GS because it is a really heavy load.

I know that all of that is a lot of information to take in, but I just thought of you and all the advice you gave during the ACT class so I thought I'd ask for some help. I'm really torn and I know that in a few weeks I'll need to have a decision made, my stomach is upset just from typing all of that! It makes me nervous to think about. I tried to give you all of the facts and my honest opinions. Please let me know what you think!!

Thanks so much! -Mindy

Mindy,

Thanks for the email and I apologize for the late response. The snow day radically threw off my week (who plans for a snow day in late March?). I have read your email six times because there is a lot of information.

First, both schools are great. I have had students attend both schools. I have personally never visited TCU but have been on the campus of Kentucky.

Second, forget your boyfriend and what others might say. Kentucky is a great school whether your boyfriend goes there or not.

Third, TCU makes me a little nervous when you stated that your friend spends all her summer money on her sorority. That's a big red flag. Multiply that over four years, and it sounds like your friend is going to spend $10K+ on a sorority. It gives the impression that there may be a "keeping up with the Jones" pressure on campus...

Fourth, Lexington is a fantastic city and most likely provides great internships to UK. You would be hard pressed to have a city – or state – that has more school spirit than Kentucky. UK is a big deal down there. TCU probably has great school spirit as well, but the entire state spreads their enthusiasm out among Texas and professional teams. In Kentucky it is Kentucky or Louisville. That's it!

Fifth, the loan amount difference is equivalent to a nice car or down payment on a home. You need to think about that. College is wonderful, but you need to start thinking about life after college.

Sixth, be thankful that you are choosing between two great schools. You've earned it through years of hard work!

Let me know if that helps!

Jason

Hi Jason,

Just wanted to let you know I chose Kentucky! You had a lot of good advice that made me think twice about spending a ton of money on an overpriced school. Plus, UK is a fantastic University with plenty of opportunities! I can't wait to be there next fall... Thank you again!!

-Mindy

That was a lot of information. However, I am sharing this exchange because Mindy's thought process was right on: she focused on the cost. Notice how much she knew about scholarships, expenses, etc. It wasn't just mom and dad looking at the numbers: Mindy knew exactly what her parents were going to contribute and that was it. It was up to Mindy to cover the difference.

Mindy and her parents attended one of my parent seminars prior to her senior year. Notice that dad spoke to both schools about getting more money for Mindy. One school said no, the other gave her $12,000 more ($3,000 per year). My point is that he asked. The first school said no but that did not deter him from asking the second school, and that one little question made the difference because Mindy chose Kentucky.

As I am typing this I have tears in my eyes. I know Mindy because she was one of my ACT students. I am very proud of her.

This is not the 60s, 70s, 80s, or 90s. This is the 21st Century and the concept of an affordable college education is not the same as it was back then. Now, society is asking a 17 year old to buy a college education that is the equivalent of purchasing a house and a used car on the same day. How many of you would feel comfortable with that? College is a major financial investment for most families and it needs to be approached as such: an investment with no guarantee of complete return, with financial risks that need to be considered. This concept leads into the next part: The Dream School.

Chapter 3

The Dream School

One summer I had a student in class named Austin. Austin was a near perfect high school student. He was a straight A student who took as many honors classes and AP courses as he could work into his schedule, a good athlete, and enjoyed doing community service.

It was the summer between his sophomore and junior year of high school. He wanted to get a head start on preparing for the ACT. I later learned that this "head start" work ethic was nothing new with Austin. According to his mom, ever since he was ten years old he always wanted to go to the University of Notre Dame. That was his dream school and he spent eight years preparing for it.

Most of my summer ACT students take the September ACT. Since Austin was a soccer player and the Illinois high school season is in the fall, he waited to take his first ACT test in October of his junior year. He scored a 30. Most students would have been thrilled but not Austin. That score may have been good for 99 percent of the colleges in America, but he had his sight set on Notre Dame.

Once his soccer season was over, Austin took the rest of my fall semester ACT classes. After Christmas Break, he took my spring semester ACT classes. One day I asked him why he decided to take my classes three times. Did he really like me that much? His response was simple: "I want to know as much about the ACT as you do." I cannot overemphasize how focused he was.

He took the National April ACT and scored a 33. Two weeks later he participated in the PSAE ACT given to all public school juniors in the State of Illinois and increased his score to a 35. Austin felt this score was good enough for Notre Dame. With the exception of not scoring a perfect on the ACT, Austin had a flawless academic record. Now, he was on to the next step: applying to Notre Dame.

For those of you not familiar with top tier schools like Notre Dame, Northwestern University, Washington University in St. Louis, and Ivy League school, you cannot just complete a college application and mail it off. That will almost certainly guarantee an instant rejection. You have to visit these schools, the admissions office meets you, they meet your parents, you give them a list of references, and these schools contact those people. Top tier schools want the best of the best. These requirements were okay with Austin and his family. They were ready and did everything necessary prior to applying. Once those important tasks were completed, the application was submitted.

Not long after Christmas Break, Austin received his acceptance letter from Notre Dame. He and his family were so excited. His eight years of preparation and focus on his dream school was about to become a reality. The only piece of information needed from Notre Dame was Austin's scholarship offer.

Although Austin wanted to go to Notre Dame, he did apply to other universities, which is something I emphasize in my ACT class. We are familiar with the phrase "don't put all your eggs into one basket." Students need to have back-up schools just in case something unexpectedly happens. As winter turned to spring, Austin's list of back-up schools would be narrowed down to one. However, that did not matter to Austin; he was going to Notre Dame.

As the weeks went on, Austin was getting more excited, but his mom was getting nervous. Every school had sent acceptance letters and then a scholarship offer. It was now late March/early April and no scholarship package had arrived from Notre Dame, so his mom decided to call.

NOTE: Your student should have a contact person at every school they are considering. That way the family is always going through the same person. This not only speeds up the process of getting necessary information but also creates an advocate for your student in the admissions office – someone that truly knows your student and your family. This way your student is not a piece of paper (college application) but a real person.

His mom called their contact, they exchanged pleasantries, and the mom asked about the scholarship package. The following is the exchange according to Austin's mom:

ND: "Austin is not getting a scholarship. Who told you Austin would get a scholarship?"

At this point, his mom was shocked. She did not understand. Austin had a near perfect academic record, so it must have been something else. His mom asked if there was something wrong with his essays, interview, meetings, references, etc.

ND: "Austin is a great student. We are looking forward to having him on campus. He will be in the engineering honors program, so you know he's one of the top students coming next year."

Now Austin's mom was really confused. He's was going to be one of the top admitted students, but he was not going to receive a scholarship? Sensing mom's frustration, the representative responds:

ND: "I don't think you understand. We are the University of Notre Dame. We don't have to give out academic scholarships."

Austin's mom was shocked, but the representative is correct: Notre Dame does not need to give academic scholarships. Neither does Northwestern University, Washington University in St. Louis, or the Ivy League schools. They may give out financial aid packages made up of grants and scholarships if they choose, but they do not have the more structured level like the rest of the colleges across the country, because many families are willing to pay full price to send their children to top tier schools. For most, merely getting accepted to these schools is the ultimate prize – the end of the journey. That's how Austin felt as well, but his mom and dad had other thoughts.

QUICK STORY: A doctor from the Chicago area recently attended one of my parent seminars. During the break and after I had shared the Austin story, he told me the following about one of his colleagues. His friend's son was on the wait list at Notre Dame, so the dad contacted the Notre Dame Admissions Office and offered to make a sizeable donation to the school if that would help get his son into Notre Dame. The Notre Dame Representative responded:

"Thanks for the offer, but we have over one hundred students on the wait list whose families have already donated more than $10 million and their kids are still on the list."

These are students from families (legacies) that have been donating money to Notre Dame for decades.

The above story illustrates two important points:

1. Families are willing to donate a lot of money to get their students into top tier schools.

2. Top tier schools are highly selective and do not necessarily make admissions decisions based on a student's family's bank account.

DISCLAIMER: *This story was shared by a parent. I cannot confirm the numbers; however, they do not surprise me. I have known many parents that were willing to donate a great deal of money in order to "help" their student get into a specific university.*

Austin's back up school came down to one clear choice: Southern Illinois University in Carbondale, IL. Most are shocked to hear that because SIU seems so far from Notre Dame in regard to prestige.

There were two reasons why SIUC was his second choice. The first and most important was that he received a full-ride scholarship. However, Austin still wanted to go to Notre Dame.

Most students would be thrilled to have a free college education. This is why I am sharing this particular story. Austin was very intelligent and very conservative, but this was his DREAM SCHOOL. This happens a lot to high school seniors. They get so focused on their dream school that objectivity goes to the wayside. Dream schools blind students and families. I cannot tell you how many times I have heard the following:

"I want to go there no matter what."

"We will do whatever takes to get our child into that school."

This was Austin's mindset and like most families the final decision would be Austin's decision. The reality is that parents cannot pick a college for their student. Most students, when they go to college are 18 years old and classified as legal adults. It needs to be their decision. If not, a family runs the risk of the student dropping out or transferring, which can make the college years more challenging.

However, the student needs guidance from parents – a lot of guidance – because I guarantee your student is getting a lot of advice from other 17 and 18 year old students that they spend 40 plus hours a week with at school. This was happening to Austin. All his friends were telling him to go to his dream school. After all, gaining acceptance from Notre Dame is an honor. It was at this moment his mom did something that all parents need to do: compute the real cost of college.

Austin and his mom sat down at the computer and created an Excel file to find out how much Notre Dame was really going to cost. At this time, I need to provide additional information. Austin was going to study engineering and planned on going directly to graduate school. His mom took this into account.

Most students do not receive a scholarship, their parents cannot contribute much (Austin's situation), and they do not have much savings of their own. Where does the money for college come from? The answer is student loans. Your student is going to hear the following statement multiple times:

"The interest rates on student college loans are LOW..."

At the time of this writing our country is currently in a recession (despite what political leaders claim) and loan interest rates are low on EVERYTHING: home mortgage, car loans, department store payment plans, etc. It does not matter. A loan is still a loan. It must be paid back.

In our country when an adult declares bankruptcy, typically all loans can be forgiven except college loans. College loans must be paid back because in the end they are directly or indirectly connected to the government.

College loans tend to have extensions in order to pay back the loan. Usually, student loan payments begin within six months of graduation in order to give recent graduates an opportunity to find a job. However, many graduates still have not found a job or are underemployed. Not a problem. Many of these lending institutions will make the loan payback period longer in order to lower the monthly payment. This usually sounds good to a recent college graduate.

Because Austin would have loans covering six years of college, his mother computed the loan repayment length at 30 years using the current interest rates at that particular time. This produced a monthly payment that seemed reasonable to Austin. Most families who would have taken the time to do this would stop at the monthly payment which looks so reasonable.

However, Austin's mom took one more important step: she added all the interest payments during the life of the loan and the original loan amount. The day Austin would complete graduate school at the age of 23 years old, he would owe over $500,000.

When I share this story in my ACT classes immediately many students start looking at the last table and are confused. How could he end up owing over half a million dollars? This is why parents need to be involved, because most of us currently have or have had major loans in our life, usually a home mortgage. Most high school students have no concept of debt, especially in large amounts. The following is an example I share with students to help them understand.

If a family buys a home that requires a $250,000 home mortgage and at an interest rate of 5% (I know that seems high now but interest rates will not stay low forever) on a 30 year fixed mortgage then the bank would end up getting just under $230,000 in interest.

When Austin saw how much he owed, he decided to go to SIUC and told his mom the following:

"I can't afford to go to Notre Dame."

Austin's mom called to share this story for two reasons. One, she wanted me to warn my students about Notre Dame. I need to point out that there is nothing wrong with Notre Dame. Notre Dame has a very low acceptance rate because so many students want to attend and are willing to pay full price. Interested students just need to be aware that they, like Austin, may be expected to pay for everything.

Two, she asked me to call Austin because he was a little down about the whole ordeal. That's understandable; he was not going to attend his number one choice. As stated earlier, parents need to help students from getting too emotionally connected to dream schools. Happy endings always occur in fairy tales, not necessarily life.

I did call Austin to first congratulate him on his decision. Any time a student gets a full-ride academic scholarship offer regardless of the size or school that is a big deal. The fact that he got a full-ride academic scholarship was even more impressive.

I also wanted to share something with him because I understood what he was thinking but wasn't saying over the phone.

Jason: "Austin, most people would say Notre Dame is a better school than SIUC, right?"

Austin: "Yes."

Jason: "It's not, but most people would say that."

Austin: "How can you say that?"

I went on to explain. As a public school teacher I attended my fair share of high school graduation ceremonies. I really don't like them, because they are very superficial. We need to be honest: is anyone really worried about not graduating from high school? You really have to try hard NOT to graduate. The No Child Left Behind Act encourages schools to do whatever it takes to get students through graduation, and most schools follow suit. In case you don't believe me, the current national high school graduation rate is hovering around 80%. The percent moves into the upper 90s when inner-city schools and their student bodies are removed from the calculations.

As a teacher you usually know every student or at least know of them. There have been times I have had tears in my eyes while watching a student receive their diploma because I saw them develop from a confused freshman to a senior truly ready for their next step in life. As teachers and parents we cherish those students. It's the student walking behind that makes our stomach turn.

The next student is not walking, he is strutting. He is motioning to the crowd although all graduates were told not to. You know where his relatives are sitting because they are screaming even though all spectators have been told to be quiet through the duration of the presentation of diplomas. However, they can't help it. After all, they never expected to be at graduation, because this boy had been arrested just six months ago for a few "little" misdemeanors, was way behind in school, but SOMEHOW it all worked out and he graduated (true story).

Both students walked across the stage. Both shook the hand of the same school board president and then the hand of the same principal as they were handed diplomas that look exactly the same. They attended the same school, had access to the same teachers, same courses, same curriculum, but did they receive the same education? Absolutely not.

A school does not make a student. A student's education or experience is based on opportunities they choose – or choose not – to take advantage of. There are endless opportunities at every college in America, that it is simply impossible to take advantage of them all. Do you want to study abroad? Many community colleges offer these very same programs? Why spend $30,000 at a four-year university to study overseas when a community college may be offering the same program for a fraction of the cost?

And this brings us to the second reason why SIUC was Austin's back-up school. At the time Austin was looking at schools, SIUC was able to offer him something that Notre Dame could not: an internship opportunity as a freshman. SIUC had a smaller engineering program, while all of the internships at Notre Dame went to upper classmen.

Austin received a paid internship with a national company the summer after his freshmen year of college. He did so well that the company offered him a job despite that fact that he had not even started his second year of college. The job offer was a guaranteed position once he graduated from college as well as paid internships the next two summers. When Austin finished his undergraduate degree, he decided not to pursue a master's degree but rather begin his career with another company that offered to pay for his graduate school if he chose to pursue it in the future.

Looking back, I guarantee you that Austin would tell all my students and parents that he is glad he went to SIUC for free as opposed to owing over a half a million dollars for a "label" degree. More importantly, Austin and his family could not have predicted what would happen to our country.

I made a point not to mention dates until now. Austin graduated from high school in May of 2007, the same year our country reached its economic peak with no indication that the economy would change any time soon. Austin graduated from college in May of 2011, the same year the Occupy Wall Street movement began. For those of you that have forgotten, the movement included a large portion of college graduates who could not find a job but possessed massive college debt. Consider the following statistics[11,12].

Unemployment Rate for Recent College Graduates	
1998	1.9%
2011	12.6%

That's the difference between the late 20th Century and the new reality of college graduates.

As you go through the college journey with your student, continue to point them to life after college. I tell all my students that they need to sit down with their parents and discuss finances. Students need to know what financial support if any they can expect from their parents. Parents need to be honest.

Parents before you have this conversation with your student, I strongly encourage you to do the calculations and determine what is realistic in regard to family contributions to your student's education. Have the numbers already worked out, so you can show your student. Explain to your student your family budget and make it clear that the amount is what it is. In short, draw the line in the sand.

I had a girl attempt to do this with her mom, but mom did not want to discuss the topic. The girl repeatedly wanted to discuss it because the family was having a rough time financially, and the girl just wanted to have an honest conversation. Parent, if your student is mature enough to go to college, then they are mature enough to learn about the family finances regardless of the family's situation. The girl was in tears as she was sharing the above with me and kept asking me what she should do.

"Keep going to your parents and ask them to sit down and talk about it. The sooner you do this, the better your entire family will feel."

I have begun with college costs. I do this in my ACT classes as well. I have had students tell me that this does not apply to them because their parents are paying for everything. My response usually is the following:

"Really? Everything? What's everything? My dad went to the U of I in 1970 and everything was under $1,000. It's not $1,000 anymore. Your *everything* and your parents' *everything* may not be a college's *everything*."

The number one reason students drop out of college is because they run out of money, in part, because they don't really know how expensive college is and neither do most parents. Start with the finances. Be realistic. Have the family meeting. It may be hard or uncomfortable, but you will be glad you did.

I have had over 50 students pass up full academic scholarships in order to attend top tier schools. Personally, I do not understand why someone would do this. These were highly intelligent students who worked incredibly hard in school for years. Their parents were college educated and had a history of being actively involved in their child's education. However, the families got caught up in the "dream school" philosophy. That was their choice. However, I think it would be hard to justify declining a free college undergraduate education and pay over $200,000 for a similar degree with no guarantee of better opportunities AFTER college. Students and families need to think about life after school. College is simply a stepping stone in life; a tool; don't make it bigger than that.

Chapter 4

College Rankings

There is a perception in the country that certain colleges and universities are just better than others. Millions of parents every year buy publications that "rank" these institutions. However, few question how the rankings are determined.

I recommend all parents read the following books:

Crazy U: *One Dad's Crash Course in Getting His Kid into College*
By Andrew Ferguson

Higher Education? *How Colleges are Wasting Our Money and Failing Our Kids – And What We Can Do About It*
By Andrew Hackerer & Claudia Dreifus

The first was written by a journalist who chronicles his experience helping his son through the college selection process. He actually investigated how the "rankings" are determined. You will learn as he did that the rankings are highly subjective, have little merit, and are compiled on an annual basis mainly because it is a highly profitable business for publishing companies.

Let me provide an example that will help high school students. Every year our country celebrates March Madness in men's college basketball. For half the year, we have "experts" telling us which teams and conferences are the best. Then a special committee is assigned to rank the teams using the latest in technology to truly analyze where teams should be placed in the brackets. And yet, every year there are major upsets despite all the attention given to men's college basketball.

My point is the following: more time and attention is given to men's college basketball than ranking actual colleges and universities. It's not possible to accurately rank schools and Ferguson's book reveals the truth behind rankings.

Employers cannot hire a university; they hire the best individuals they can find based on what they have accomplished in the real world, not necessarily in the classroom. College rankings do little to help employers locate individuals to hire.

We want our students to have the best possible college professors. Unfortunately, the "best" professors may not be actually teaching undergraduate courses and that is revealed in *Higher Education?* Hacker spent over three years actually visiting the top tier colleges. One of the biggest complaints he heard from students was that they worked hard in high school to get into a top school, spent a lot of money on their college education, and then when they arrived they were being taught by graduate assistants or part-time professors not much older than the students.

Many of the professors you see on those cable news shows are not teaching undergraduate classes but rather doing research, writing books, and teaching a few graduate courses. I worked in the college textbook industry for a while and had the opportunity to work with one of the top authors in the country. He graduated from college before turning 20 years old. When I met him back in the mid-90s, he was teaching one class at Villanova University and making $400,000. Why?

He was a well-known author, so his books were on college campuses around the country. He did a lot of speaking engagements and his name was connected to the university. In short, he was an advertising tool; it was better to have him do things other than teach.

It's not possible to predict who will be teaching your student at any college, especially the first two years. The bigger the school, the more likely it will be a professor presenting in a larger lecture hall to hundreds of students with small discussion groups taught by teaching assistants during your student's first two years. The smaller the school, the more likely a student will have a professor presenting to a class of 50 or less students. In a community college, the size of the class most likely will be less than 30 students with an instructor who only teaches and is typically not required to do research or professional writing like major university professors.

Every year one can find research showing that the name of the university is one of the last things an employer looks at when interviewing recent college graduates. Employers do not care where a student went to school, but rather what a student accomplished WHILE in school. This is where work experience and internships become very important. Consider the following research: the first was completed in 2007 and the second.

In 2007 the top ten factors employers looked for in a recent college graduate were:

1. The ability to work well in teams—especially with people different from yourself

2. An understanding of science and technology and how these subjects are used in real-world settings

3. The ability to write and speak well

4. The ability to think clearly about complex problems

5. The ability to analyze a problem to develop workable solutions

6. An understanding of global context in which work is now done

7. The ability to be creative and innovative in solving problems

8. The ability to apply knowledge and skills in new settings

9. The ability to understand numbers and statistics

10. A strong sense of ethics and integrity

Source: "How Should Colleges Prepare Students to Succeed in Today's Global Economy?" (Results of a national poll by Peter D. Hart Research Associates, 2007).

In August 2013, Harris Interactive conducted a survey of 1,000 hiring managers. The following are the top three things that made a recent college graduate job applicant attractive as a prospective employee according to the hiring managers[13]:

1. 93% wanted evidence that the prospective employee could lead.

2. 91% thought it was important that prospective employees participated in extracurricular activities related to their field of study.

3. 82% wanted to see a completed a formal internship before the applicant graduated from college.

Notice that neither study stated that the name of the college was important to a potential employer. I encourage you to review the results of both studies with your high school student BEFORE, DURING, and AFTER their college years.

Leadership roles in campus organizations, on athletic teams, or jobs are very important as well. Employers don't just want workers; they often want future leaders for their company.

Chapter 5

College Graduation Rates

Six years to get a four year degree?

If you would ask most Illinois parents and high school students to pick one word to describe SIUC, the most frequent response would be the following: party. For decades, SIUC has been known as a party school. Take a moment to look at the following table.

How long it really takes to get a "Four Year" Degree		
College/University	4 years	6 years
Bradley University	53%	75%
Eastern Illinois University	32%	59%
Illinois College	48%	57%
Illinois State University	44%	71%
Illinois Wesleyan University	77%	82%
MacMurray College	22%	36%
Millikin University	54%	65%
Northern Illinois University	26%	56%
Northwestern University	86%	94%
Olivet Nazarene University	44%	56%
Southern Illinois University	24%	44%
University of Illinois (C-U)	66%	82%
Washington University	86%	93%
Western Illinois University	30%	53%

Source: U.S. Department of Education Institute of Education Sciences
http://nces.ed.gov/collegenavigator/

Let me make sure the table is clear. In every group of 100 freshmen to attend SIUC (Southern Illinois University), only 24 will graduate four years later at SIUC. The six year column is not referring to graduate school; it means six years to get a four-year degree. SIUC is still under 50 percent. Students are having so much fun that they are not leaving.

Take a moment and look at the other schools on the list. Many are not doing much better than SIUC. The gem of our state, the University of Illinois, has a four year graduation rate of 66 percent. To put it another way, one out of every three students that attend the U of I as a freshman does not graduate from the U of I four years later. That's not encouraging either.

The rates are much lower than what they were in the last 20th Century. You need to know what is going on so this does not happen to your student.

The above table does not account for students who transfer from or to a school. Unfortunately, it is impossible for schools or the government to track transfer students.

I have studied graduation rates and here are some basic, unsurprising patterns.

1. The more expensive the school, the higher the graduation rate. I suspect parents are making sure students are taking advantage of their investment.

2. The schools with the higher standards, i.e. Northwestern University and Washington University, the higher the graduation rates. Top high school students are ready for the rigors of college. They also tend to have better study habits, understand how to perform on tests, already can read at the college level, and possess more self-discipline than the typical incoming college freshmen found at most other colleges. They are also less likely to transfer.

In class I use a simple illustration that has proven very effective: Joe and Emily.

Coming out of high school, Joe and Emily are the same: same grades, same ACT score, and same class rank. They both decide to attend the same university and study the same program. On paper, they are academic twins. However, when they arrive on campus they have different goals.

Joe has three goals:

1. Get good grades. His parents and teachers have taught him for years that grades are important and they are. They provide immediate feedback on classroom performance.

2. Never have class before noon. This is possible. Most schools offer classes through the day and evening, which is ideal for students who need to work during the day, but that's not why Joe is doing it. Goal #2 goes with #3.

3. Joe dated the same girl in high school all four years. She's back home and eventually wants to get married. Joe is not sure, so he wants to play the field and date three different girls at the same time. Is this possible? If a boy has enough organizational skills and no morals, then it is possible but not recommended.

Emily has two goals:

1. Get good grades just like Joe.

2. Graduate as soon as possible in order to minimize the cost of college.

They both attend summer orientation where classes and schedules are determined. Students soon learn that colleges treat them like adults. After all, incoming college students usually are 18 years old. They both pick out their classes. Joe will take 12 credit hours and Emily will take 18 (for the remainder of the illustration I will just refer to credit hours simply as hours).

Student	Freshmen Year
Joe	12
Emily	18

I am using the credit hour plan that is most common in our country. A few colleges may be different. However, the lesson provided via the illustration applies to ALL colleges.

Let me explain what these numbers mean. The typical high school student is in school seven hours a day, five days a week, totaling 35 hours a week. "12" means Joe is in class 12 hours a week. That means his schedule could be classes on Mondays, Wednesdays, and Fridays from 12 noon to 4 pm with no classes on Tuesdays and Thursdays. Joe's living the dream and still considered a full-time student.

We will assume Emily is a morning student. Her schedule could be classes on Mondays, Wednesdays, and Fridays from 8 am to 12 noon and classes on Tuesdays and Thursdays from 9 am to 12 noon. That's a great schedule, too. What's the deal? Why are high school students in class so much and college students in class so little?

The difference deals with work outside of class. For every hour a college student is in class they are expected to do two hours of studying for that particular hour. Joe would then have 12 hours of class plus 24 hours of studying totaling 36 hours of school. Emily would have 18 hours of class plus 36 hours of studying totaling 54 hours of class. This is why most colleges limit hours to 18 per semester (unless the student is in a performance major like music or drama).

Colleges treat their students like adults so no one is verifying that students are actually studying two hours for every hour of class time. This would lead to whole another chapter, but we will not address that topic in this book.

Joe's 36 hours would still be less than a college-bound high school student. These students typically study 10 to 15 hours a week, making their school week 45 to 50 hours a week. That's more than Joe. I need to point out that what Joe is doing is perfectly acceptable and he is maintaining full-time student status.

They both complete their freshman fall semester with straight As and make the Dean's List. Their parents are proud. Both succeeded, so there is no need to change anything. They do the same thing again the next three semesters.

For most college freshmen the fall semester is simply about surviving because college is so different from high school. College truly is a different world. It's very important that parents "keep an eye" on their student during that freshmen fall semester.

Student	**Freshmen Year**		**Sophomore Year**	
Joe	12	12	12	12
Emily	18	18	18	18

After two years of college, Joe and Emily both have straight As. They are doing great! Now it is the summer after their sophomore year. In high school the summer before the junior year, many students start thinking about life after high school: college. College is similar. Students start thinking about life after college. After all, they are half way done just like they were in high school. And this is where many college students get into trouble.

College is not high school. High school is based on years not credits. High schools do use a "credit" system, but I have never had a student in my ACT classes worried about having enough credits to graduate from high school. College is different. College is based on credits earned, not years.

At this point in our story, Joe has 48 hours while Emily has 72 hours. She is already one year ahead of Joe's pace. If she continues at this rate, she will graduate in 3 ½ years and Joe will take six years. Those two extra years are not free. We will assume they are attending a college that locks the cost for four years (some colleges actually do this).

Total Cost of College			
Joe	6 years	$30,000 per year	$180,000
Emily	3 ½ years	$30,000 per year	$105,000

They went to the same school and completed the same program but did not pay the same price. Here's where things have changed since the 20th Century:

Which student does the university like today?
That would be Joe.

Many college admissions officers would argue that point, so let me expand on it. No college is making Joe go six years or even encouraging it. However, I am not aware of any colleges publicly denouncing students that take longer than four years either. I don't know of any schools warning high school students and parents about their low graduation rates. Do you?

There are programs within some colleges that tend to be stricter than others due to the nature of their field such as pre-med, pre-vet, architecture, and engineering. If students are not keeping up then the department may potentially have the student transfer to another degree program within the school.

Why would Joe take fewer classes when he is actually paying for 18 hours each semester? He's attempting to protect goal #1: get good grades. Joe and Emily both received academic scholarships worth $10,000 per year. The scholarship was automatically renewable as long as they kept their grade point average at a certain level. Joe was ensuring he would get the good grades by taking fewer classes and it "worked," or so he thought.

Total Scholarship Package			
Joe	6 years	$10,000 per year	$60,000
Emily	3 ½ years	$10,000 per years	$35,000

The above numbers are wrong. Academic scholarships typically only last four years. They both receive $40,000. Joe is not rewarded for taking longer and Emily is not punished for graduating early. This happened to me. I graduated in December and was sent a check for $5,000 the following January. It was a pleasant surprise.

Not every school would automatically give Emily a check for $5,000. If your student is going to graduate early, bring that to the attention of the school, and request (demand) that the full amount of the scholarship be applied during the fall semester. Some schools may say "no" while others may work with you.

Every year students get a bill from their respective schools. The bills typically show the total costs minus scholarships and grants. The remaining total can then be covered by loans or cash on hand. For the sake of the illustration, we are not going to incorporate a loan.

Joe's Total Cost		
Freshman Year	$30,000 - $10,000 scholarship	= $20,000
Sophomore Year	$30,000 - $10,000 scholarship	= $20,000
Junior Year	$30,000 - $10,000 scholarship	= $20,000
Senior Year	$30,000 - $10,000 scholarship	= $20,000

The family is not surprised. They knew they would have to come up with $20,000. Again, we will assume this is a school that locks the costs of college (not all schools do this).

He is now supposed to be done with college, but he is not even close. In the spring of his senior year, he will be contacted by the college. The contact will make the following points:

1. Joe, you have not completed your program; therefore, you will not be graduating in May.

2. Joe, if you plan on completing the program, you must complete these courses (a list will be provided).

3. Joe, because you did not finish in four years, you have lost your academic scholarship.

4. Joe, because you did not finish in four years and if you choose to return, you will now need to pay the same cost as next fall's incoming freshmen class: $40,000.

Joe was expecting $20,000 AND his parents were not expecting anything!

Joe's Total Cost		
Freshman Year	$30,000 - $10,000 scholarship	= $20,000
Sophomore Year	$30,000 - $10,000 scholarship	= $20,000
Junior Year	$30,000 - $10,000 scholarship	= $20,000
Senior Year	$30,000 - $10,000 scholarship	= $20,000
Fifth Year	$40,000	= $40,000
Sixth Year	$40,000	= $40,000

Where is a 21 year old going to get $40,000? Joe could ask mom and dad, but would you give that much money to a kid who messed around for four years? Most parents would not. He could get a loan but most loans also have four-year limits too. There are loans for year five and six, but the interest rates will be much higher because the student is now a risk. Every lender went to college and understands an undergraduate degree can be completed within four years. Most students get a job. Unfortunately, this takes time away from school and many eventually drop out and never return.

This is why college debt is such a serious issue. Students are not getting done in four years. Notice the totals in the far right of the last table. The first four years cost Joe $80,000. The extra two years were an additional $80,000. In short, he ended up doubling his cost. This does not even take into account the additional interest he will need to pay because he was too busy having fun and not focusing completely on academics. Please do not take this illustration lightly and think of "Joe" as an extreme example.

> ## USA Today: June 4th, 2009 Headline
> ## 4-year colleges graduate 53% of students in 6 years

Let me translate. 47 percent of students have either transferred, dropped out, or are continuing into a seventh year. "Joe" is really an average Joe. Your student is going to go to college with a lot of Joes who will be telling your student to not take that class, withdraw from that class, or just skip a class and have fun.

Please share the following with your student (i.e. drill it into their heads):

> *Every time you don't sign up for a class that fits into your schedule,*
> *you already paid for it and you don't get your money back.*

> *Every time you withdraw from a class,*
> *you already paid for it and you don't get your money back.*

> *Every time you skip a class,*
> *you already paid for it and you don't get your money back.*

Let me put the previous examples in dollar amounts that will help a student better understand the costs of college using two well-known schools and their respective 2012 – 2013 total cost numbers.

2012 – 2013 Total Costs	Don't sign up or withdraw from class	Skip one class one day
University of Illinois	$2,388	$50
Northwestern University	$5,070	$106

In the past, I had a student tell me that he really didn't want to go to college; he just wanted to get out of the house and be a man. There is nothing wrong with that but don't go to college because that's not being an adult. College is still a somewhat protective environment; it's not exactly the real world. Some students should consider a gap year in order to determine what they really want to do. Work for a year and learn what the real world is really like. Consider the military. Mission work can also teach priceless life lessons. All of those can help anyone grow up quickly.

When I mentioned those options to this student, he told me that I didn't understand. He wanted to go to college in order to experience college life; he just didn't want to go to the college classes. I was dumbfounded by his blunt honesty, so I suggested the following: get an apartment on the campus of the University of Illinois and pretend to be a student. That's a lot better than paying to go to the U of I and not being a student like the apparent 18% that were unable to graduate with a four-year degree in six years. Some students are just not ready for the responsibility required to be successful at a four-year college.

Let me end this section with one more sobering headline article from USA Today.

USA Today: July 2nd, 2013 Headline

Too high a price for education?

Students less likely to graduate than to default on loans at some colleges

College is a major financial investment. However, all financial investments come with a risk with no guarantee of return. College is no different. Please make sure your student understands what happens if they default on their college loans: lower credit scores, higher interest rates on credit cards, may not be able to get a car loan, and most likely would not be able to get a mortgage.

Chapter 6

Financial Lesson

We need to take the Joe and Emily example one step further. Too often college students miss out on a very important factor when considering the costs associated with taking longer than four years to earn an undergraduate degree: lost income.

The national starting salary average for a college graduate is approximately $45,000.[14] Based on the Joe and Emily scenario, here is what happened.

Joe's undergraduate education was supposed to cost him $80,000. Instead Joe graduated in six years, taking on $80,000 in additional college costs. At the age of 23 years old, Joe has $160,000 of debt and no work experience.

Emily graduated from college early, so her college costs totaled $70,000. Since she graduated early, she was able to work an extra half year. Assuming she only made $45,000 per year, she earned $112,500 during the 2 ½ year period following her college graduation.

23 years old Financial Picture
"Should have been" Joe
$80,000 in college debt
2 years of college work experience
$90,000 in earnings
+$10,000
"Reality" Joe
$160,000 in college debt
No work experience
No earnings
- $160,000
Emily
$70,000 in college debt
2 ½ years of work experience
$112,500 in earnings
+$42,500

This is a simplistic model but demonstrates not only the importance of graduating on time, but the importance of developing a solid financial foundation at a young age. As a reminder, Joe and Emily were the same in high school in regard to academic performance. They went to the same college and pursued the same degree program. However, they did not end up in the same position at the age of 23 years old. Be careful!

Chapter 7

Catching Up & Getting Ahead
The Community College Advantage

Joe did not graduate on time because he was only taking 12 credit hours per semester. Most college programs require 120 credit hours to graduate. That means a student needs to average 15 credit hours per semester. This assumes that the student does not change their college major.

One of the best ways to stay on pace to graduate from college is to take advantage of community colleges. Community colleges serve two primary purposes:

1. Provide technical training and certification programs that only require two years of study.

2. Provide a strong transition from high school to a four-year university by providing lower level general education courses that can easily be transferred.

Students can start taking community college courses as soon as they turn 16 years old. I encourage all of my ACT students to do just that. Consider the following scenario.

Getting Ahead with Community Colleges

- High School Junior Year
- Summer – take 6 credit hours at local community college
- High School Senior Year
- Summer – take 6 credit hours at local community college
- Four – Year College Freshman Year
- Summer – take 6 credit hours at local community college
- Four – Year College Sophomore Year
- Four – Year College Junior Year
- Four – Year College Senior Year – *graduate in December*

18 Community College credit hours
one full semester at a Four – Year College

21st Century technology has made it even easier to take community college courses as many can now be completed online. Many area high schools offer dual-credit classes which count as high school and college courses. However, the biggest advantage is the money saved.

Community College Advantage	
Community Colleges in Illinois	**2012 – 2013 Tuition & Fees**
Danville Area Community College	$3,525
Heartland Community College	$4,080
Illinois Central College	$3,195
Kankakee Community College	$3,390
Lake Land College	$3,024
Lincoln Land Community College	$2,568
Parkland College	$3,360
Richland Community College	$3,042

Source: U.S. Department of Education Institute of Education Sciences
http://nces.ed.gov/collegenavigator/

Compare those numbers to the four year universities in previously supplied tables. Community college is a very cost effective way to dramatically lower the total cost of a college education either by taking community college courses as soon as you can or beginning at a community college right after high school. Consider the following scenarios with the University of Illinois and Parkland College.

Taking advantage of Community Colleges

SCENARIO #1:

2009 – 2010	U of I and Live on Campus	$25,110
2010 – 2011	U of I and Live on Campus	$26,538
2011 – 2012	U of I and Live on Campus	$27,628
2012 – 2013	U of I and Live on Campus	<u>$28,564</u>
		$107,840

SCENARIO #2:

2009 – 2010	Parkland and Live at Home	$7,060
2010 – 2011	Parkland and Live at Home	$7,560
2011 – 2012	U of I and Live on Campus	$27,628
2012 – 2013	U of I and Live on Campus	<u>$28,564</u>
		$70,812

That is a savings of over $37,000
and the student still gets the college experience & the U of I Degree!

NOTE: "Live at Home" in the table assumes student is paying minimal rent and/or living expenses to parents. Nothing should be free for the student.

There are a few important things to remember about community colleges. One, they typically only offer lower – level general education courses. Two, most four-year universities only allow students to transfer in so many hours. This can vary from school to school. Some universities will allow 70 hours to transfer in, which means the last 50 hours must be from their institution.

Older Students provide unique classroom environment

Community colleges tend to grow when the national economy is struggling. These last five years have been no different. Many adults are going back to school. The average age of a community college student tends to be much higher than the average at a four-year university. I've seen the average age as high as 28 years old. When an 18 year old is taking a course with someone in their upper 20s, life experiences are going to be shared that will add to the learning environment. Older students take school very seriously, especially compared to older teenagers. This environment provides priceless life lessons that may not be experienced at your average four year university.

Four – Year Degrees at Community Colleges via Partnerships

Community colleges have also started to expand into offering four-year degree programs and graduate school courses via other four-year universities. My sister-in-law graduated from Eastern Illinois University with a business degree and she was only on EIU's campus once and that was when she graduated. She started at Parkland College and lived at home. EIU offers a business degree where all the courses are taught at Parkland. This allowed her to continue to live at home. She graduated from college with no loans because she saved money living at home, worked part-time throughout her college years (graduated in four years), and it is so much cheaper to do EIU through Parkland than actually attend classes at EIU.

Did this hinder her ability to get a job since she took a non-traditional route? She got a job at State Farm National Headquarters within six months of graduation.

The following is list of Parkland's partnerships with four-year universities and the number of degree programs available with the classes being taught either on Parkland's campus or online during the Spring Semester 2013. Check your local community college for similar programs.

Eastern Illinois University	4 undergraduate degrees 2 master degrees
Franklin University	32 undergraduate degrees 6 master degrees
Greenville College	1 undergraduate degree
Indiana Wesleyan University	9 undergraduate degrees 15 master degrees
Millikin University	1 undergraduate degree
Olivet Nazarene University	1 undergraduate degree
Regis University	12 undergraduate degrees
Southern Illinois University	2 undergraduate degrees
University of Illinois at Chicago	4 undergraduate degrees
University of Illinois at Springfield	7 undergraduate degrees
University of St. Francis	2 undergraduate degrees
Western Illinois University	1 undergraduate degree

Will community college credits transfer?

Certain courses usually transfer anywhere: college level English courses, college algebra and higher math courses, science lab courses (assuming you are a non-science major), psychology, sociology, and speech communications just to name a few. Community college counselors can tell you which courses will transfer to which schools. This website also has helpful information: **www.transfer.org**.

WARNING: Top tier schools like Northwestern University and Washington University, as a policy, do not accept transfer credits. They want students to do all their work at their school. Less than 5% of schools do this; however, I would suggest you ask just to be safe.

I had a student who went to Washington University to study engineering. As previously mentioned, Washington does not accept transfer hours. However, he wanted to take summer classes but he lived over three hours from St. Louis while the local community college was less than 20 minutes from his house. His mom contacted Washington to discuss the situation. He just wanted to complete lower level general education requirements.

The college official told his mom to get copy of the course outlines from the community college, Washington University would review them, and if they were equivalent to the courses at Washington, then the community college credits would be accepted. The student's mom got the course outlines, Washington reviewed them, and all three summer courses were accepted. That totaled nine credit hours. It was a savings of almost $10,000 by taking those three courses at the community college as opposed to Washington University.

Colleges have a lot of rules, but they are really guidelines and the right official has the authority to override a rule if it makes sense. Again, never be afraid to ask questions. You might be surprised by the response you receive.

Community College & Graduation Rates

The University of Illinois and Parkland Community College are just a few miles from each other. Both will tell you the same thing: students who start at Parkland College and then transfer to the University of Illinois are much more likely to graduate in four years with a degree from the University of Illinois than someone who starts at the University of Illinois. I suspect similar relationships between community colleges and four-year universities can be found across the country.

Community colleges cannot guarantee the above. However, they provide an opportunity for students to develop a solid college education foundation without all the hoopla associated with most four year schools. There are less distractions and most community college students transfer to a four year school with little or no college loans accumulated during the first two years. That's a big deal, especially given the current state of our nation's economy.

Useless Classes

The bigger the college the more likely there will be courses that are fun or interesting but serve no purpose. Every school has at least a few courses like this. The irony is that many college students flock to these courses because "everybody is doing it," it is an easy A, or "I just need more hours!"

These courses are not free. A useless course replaces a needed course. It's that simple. Make sure your student understands this. They are in college to learn material that truly matters. Do not assume your student will be wise when creating their schedule. In fact, if you are financially assisting your student then you are an investor and have every right to review and approve their schedules. If your student does not honor your input, then let them know you will retract your investment and allow the student to truly be financially independent.

These courses are also tempting because they are easier and allow students to protect their grade point average. Students learn in high school which classes and teachers are easier; college is no different. However, this time students too often do not realize they are literally taking money out of their very own pocket in order to pad their grades. That's a problem.

The following is a small sample of useless courses offered at some of the most expensive and prestigious universities in the country.

Medieval Studies: Knights of Old & Harry Potter
School: Georgetown University   Course Cost = $3,573
Total cost for the 2012-2013 academic year: $59,900 (Tuition is $42,870)

Biology: Canine Behavior
School: Brown University   Course Cost = $3,647
Total cost for the 2012-2013 academic year: $58,140 (Tuition is $43,758)

Theory and History of Video Games
School: Swarthmore College   Course Cost = $3,590
Total cost for the 2012-2013 academic year: $58,481 (Tuition is $43,080)

Cinema & Media Studies: Rock 'N' Roll in Cinema
School: Carleton College   Course Cost = $3,704
Total cost for the 2012-2013 academic year: $58,275 (Tuition is $44,445)

Technology and Culture: Virtual People
School: Stanford University   Course Cost = $3,519
Total cost for the 2012-2013 academic year: $58,846 (Tuition is $42,225)

Below is a list of fifteen more college courses found in a list online titled *15 Bizarre College Courses.*[15]

College Course Name & College/University
Zombies in Popular Media Columbia College – Chicago
Joy of Garbage Santa Clara University
Learning from YouTube Pitzer College
The Science of Harry Potter Frostburg State University
Daytime Serials: Family and Social Roles University of Wisconsin
Maple Syrup: The Real Thing Alfred University
Lady Gaga and the Sociology of Fame University of South Carolina
Underwater Basket Weaving Reed College and University of California- San Diego
Philosophy and Star Trek Georgetown University
Cyberporn and Society State University of New York
The Science of Superheroes University of California- Irvine
Popular 'Logic' on TV Judge Shows University of California
Fat Studies George Washington University
Strategy of Starcraft University of California- Berkeley
Simpsons and Philosophy University of California- Berkeley

Courses like these are offered across the country. For example, go to www.indiana.edu - the Indiana University website - and a search for the Star Trek and Religion course. You will find it under Religious Studies and it is worth three credits.

Consider the following: if your high school student came home on a Friday and told you about a great weekend workshop called **Biology: Canine Behavior** that studies why dogs bark the way they do and it only costs $3,647 to attend, would you let them go? Of course not! Why should college be any different?

Chapter 8

The ACT Test

What part does it play in the college process?

How can my student get a high enough ACT score to get into the college he wants?

I believe there is a better way to look at this. An ACT score can help a student determine which school he or she is better suited to attend. When I was a public school teacher, I taught a statistics class for a few years. My seniors set up teams to determine a topic to study. One year a group chose college graduation rates. They made arrangements to meet with a University of Illinois college professor who had been studying how to determine in high school which minority students will be successful in college. The seniors videotaped the interview. His research showed that the most reliable factor in determining college success was the ACT score regardless of ethnicity, gender, and socioeconomic status. Ironically, he asked my students not to use his name in their research. Why? Because his findings were not what those in the academic world wanted to hear.

We want to believe that grades tell the whole story. I am sorry, but they do not. The reality is grades are not fair. Grades are fair within one teacher's classroom because everyone in that classroom is being graded by the same teacher with the same criteria. That is fair. However, as soon as students walk out of the classroom, the grade is no longer "fair" in the sense that the grade from one student cannot be compared to another student from a different classroom or a different school. Schools are different, grading systems are different, curriculums are different, and teachers are different. Colleges understand this. Colleges do consider grades but keep them in perspective based on the above.

The ACT is different. On a given Saturday everyone has the same test: same questions, same choices, and the same amount of time. That is fair. That allows a university to compare a student from, say, Bloomington to a student in Champaign, Peoria, Springfield, California, Texas, Florida, Germany, and Africa. The ACT is given in over 100 different countries. It is no longer a state competition or national competition: it is an international competition. And just like an athlete prepares for athletic competition, a student needs to prepare for this competition.

The reality is that choosing a college works two ways:

1. A student chooses what schools to apply to

2. A university chooses the students they want on campus

Measurements like the ACT help make sure both the student and the university are not wasting their time.

> **EMAIL: Four point ACT score improvement gets Robert into U of I College of Business**
>
> Jason,
>
> I had a 25 on my ACT before your class, and then I improved it to a 29 after. Your suggestion to read an hour a day helped tremendously. I have been accepted to the U of I College of Business and will attend this fall. I did not receive a scholarship, but then again Illinois really doesn't have any to give. Thanks for helping me get into this competitive program!
>
> Sincerely, Robert

To get an academic scholarship, your student would need to look at schools where their ACT composite, class rank, and grade point average puts them in the top 25 percent of students at that particular university. The "lower" the college standards are, the better chances your student will receive a bigger scholarship.

How do I get my child mentally prepared for the journey?

One reason I recommend that all students take the ACT in June right after their sophomore year is to see where they stand compared to others nationally. Scores do not lie. Amanda did this a few years ago and her story confirms why this is so important for student and parents.

Amanda attended a private high school, was an A/B student, took the ACT in June right after her sophomore year and scored a 14. Her parents were shocked! She was traumatized. She immediately took my summer ACT class and then scored a 19. A five point improvement is fantastic, but her parents were still upset.

Per request, I met with Amanda and her parents to discuss the situation. I had Amanda in class and knew her scores were reflecting her ability. In my opinion, she had major reading issues and struggled remembering basic rules in English and Math. These are important skills for the ACT as well as college. So why did her parents have different expectations? Her parents just assumed she should score a 30+ because she attended a private school and got As and Bs. That's not how the system works.

At the meeting I asked specific questions about how Amanda's grades were computed at her high school. She revealed that a majority of teachers put heavy emphasis on homework completion. She was definitely a hard worker, so her homework grades were perfect; however, her test and quiz grades were very low: Cs and Ds. That explained her ACT score: high school test grades of Cs and Ds are consistent with someone scoring between a 13 and 18.

What does the above have to do with getting mentally prepared for the journey? This is why students need to take the test early: it helps set a realistic objective for the student AND parents. In the story above, after the second ACT and our meeting, Amanda's parents realized that they needed to re-examine how they were helping their daughter. They were unintentionally creating unrealistic goals for the ACT as well as college.

Once Amanda's parents accepted that this is where their daughter was at and focused on helping her with reading deficiencies and retention, then she was able to move forward. She went through my spring semester class and scored a 22 on her third attempt. I was very proud of her and so were her parents. She had improved eight total points but more importantly had dramatically increased her reading comprehension skills and became a much better test taker which helped her in her high school classes. In short, she had worked hard in order to prepare herself for college and this was reflected in her ACT score.

The ACT is the most important test a student will take in high school. It's also the most misunderstood test in high school. There is so much false information about this test that gets passed on by students, parents, teachers, and school administrators. Because I teach ACT prep classes year around, I cannot afford to be wrong. Therefore, when a student shares a "myth" with me and I am unsure, I will then call the ACT and ask. I will not give you any false information. No one in the country knows the test better than me, which is why over 9,000 students have been through my live classes and students across the country participate in my online video class. I personally take the test three times a year to remind me what students go through. I know this test like the back of my hand.

My ACT classes deal with the test specifically; in this section of the book I will focus on what the test means and how it is used. We need to begin with what the ACT numbers actually represent.

When students, parents, and even high school faculty think about the ACT score they think 20s and 30s. That's not what colleges are considering. Universities focus on the national percentile rank. The score is not just based on how your student does; it is also based on how everyone does on the same test. Standardized test developers at this level are experts. Before the test is given, they have a general idea how many questions will be missed and they are pretty accurate. It's a very precise science. And honestly, it is a little scary.

ACT Composite	National Rank
17	28th
18	34th
19	41st
TOP 50%: 20+	
20	48th
21	55th
22	62nd
23	68th
TOP 25%: 24+	
24	74th
25	79th
26	83rd
27	87th
28	91st
29	93rd
TOP 5%: 30+	
30	95th
31	97th
THE ULTIMATE NUMBER: 32	
32	98th
33	99th
34	99th
35	99th
36	99th

Percentages can vary from year to year. The above percentages are based on the high school graduates from the Classes of 2010, 2011, and 2012.

The test also has to be designed in a way that allows a college to compare students from the Class of 2014, 2015, 2016, and across all other classes. The national ACT is given six times a year and has to be designed in a way that the tests are similar. This allows students taking, say, the December ACT to be accurately compared to those taking the February, April, and June ACT tests.

It is not possible for every student to score a 20 or higher. It is not possible for every student to score a 24 or higher. It is possible for everyone to score a 36 assuming no one misses any questions but that is not realistic. The test is designed to separate students. Families need to understand this very simple concept:

The ACT works for the colleges by separating students with a simple score.

Based on this score, accept this student.
Based on another score, do not admit this student.

Based on this score, give this student a scholarship.
Based on another score, don't give this student anything.

Based on this score, give this student $10,000 per year.
Based on another score, give this student $25,000 per year.

Various scores mean certain things. In theory, when a test is given, the scores are ordered from least correct to most correct, the system goes to the middle, and whatever that number is, becomes 20. Percents then determine the other scores. Since composite scores are rounded to whole numbers the national percentile ranks seem to have somewhat strange relationships.

An ACT composite score of 20 typically divides the country in half. A score of 20 or higher means that a student can go to a four-year college - not every four-year institution just some. If a student scores below 20 that does not mean they cannot get into a four-year college, but as the previous chart shows the students national rank is much lower and the score indicates the student may be better suited to start at a community college.

An ACT composite score of 24 is a great score as it usually ranks a student in the top 25 percent in the country. That's a big deal. Research shows that students who score a 24 or higher are more likely to graduate from college in four years. A score of 24 along with a solid academic record will get a student into over 90 percent of the schools in America.

The next magic number is a composite score of 30: top 5% in the country. Many colleges and universities will require a 30 or higher to be eligible for top level scholarships or honors programs that eventually lead to more scholarships.

I have been told by numerous parents, college admissions officers, high school guidance counselors, as well as students that 32 is the ultimate number for many prestigious schools. The difference between a 32 and 36 is just a handful of questions. At this level, all students are highly academically talented. Schools will then look more in-depth at how well-rounded these particular students are.

That's the simple explanation of the scores. However, remember the following very important point:

All colleges view the scores differently. Ask each school how they use the ACT to admit students and award scholarships.

I am going to give specific examples but keep in mind schools can change their standards every year. The key is to ask the schools and make sure you have a clear understanding of what scores are needed for admissions and various scholarship packages.

One year Indiana University had an academic scholarship that started at 26, another level at 28, and then another level at 30. The University of Missouri offered a scholarship if a student had a 27, which almost eliminated the out-of-state additional tuition. One year Northern Illinois University offered scholarships at 22 and the amount increased with each additional point. Be careful: Do not assume a school will tell you how to get more money with a higher ACT.

One Memorial Day Weekend a mom called to register her son for my summer ACT classes. During the conversation the mom mentioned that they knew how important the ACT was because their older son, John, had just graduated from high school and would be attending Olivet Nazarene University next fall. Because he scored a 25 on the ACT, he was awarded an $8,000 per year scholarship. I immediately asked if he would have gotten more with a higher score. The mom was taken back; she didn't know. Her son only took the test once.

I encouraged her to call ONU on Tuesday and ask. She did and learned that if John had scored a 27 they would have awarded him an additional $4,000 per year. This did not make her happy. The family had been looking at ONU for over a year and this was never mentioned. She asked why she was never told and received the following response:

"You never asked."

Colleges want your student to come to their college and spend as much as possible. Your goal is to get your student into the college while spending as little as possible. In one sense, the college and your family are working against each other. Again, it is just like buying a house or a car. You need to negotiate and ask plenty of questions like any major business transaction.

At this point John's mom was furious as she felt information had been purposefully hidden from the family. She asked if her son took the ACT in less than two weeks (June ACT test date) and earned the additional two points, would they increase his scholarship. They said yes. Most would have assumed that ONU would have said no. After all, the son was already coming to ONU, he had already graduated from high school, and it was already summer vacation. So why did they say yes? They wanted to keep her happy. There is nothing more dangerous than an upset mom and Facebook. Besides, $4,000 is a lot of money to a family, but it is not much to a college.

11 days went by, John took the test, and went two points the wrong way. He scored a 23. His mom was not deterred. She called ONU again and made her sales pitch: this was not fair; he had less than two weeks to prepare. Jason Franklin would be teaching a summer ACT class at ONU and she wanted to know if her son took that class and then took the September ACT and earned the 27, would ONU honor it?

Most would say John's mom was pushing her luck. Her son would already be in college for almost a month by the time the September ACT test date arrived. However, ONU granted her request. Why? View it from ONU's perspective: the student just dropped his score.

The odds of him getting a 27 were not likely, so it was a good gamble and they were still keeping the mom happy. Besides, $4,000 is not much to a college.

John took my summer ACT class, went to ONU, took the September ACT, and did not score a 27. He scored a 29! That score was an even higher scholarship level: $16,000 per year. Let's review what happened:

1. John's mom made two assertive, bold phone calls.

2. John took my summer ACT class and worked very hard. There is no magic pill for this test. A student has to put in the effort to get the desired results.

3. John's scholarship package doubled going from a total of $32,000 to $64,000.

Never be afraid to ask for more money. The college may say no but at least you asked.

Setting a Goal

Let me begin with a warning: earning straight A's in high school does not mean a student will earn a 36, a 30, or even a 20. High school success does not necessarily translate into ACT or college success. Students need to have a reasonable goal for the ACT. I spend time in every ACT class helping students realize what is realistic for them.

Let's assume a student realizes that their goal is a 24 based off practice and previous test results. The following is what they would need to do in order to reach their goal. These numbers are based on the June 2012 scoring table. Every test is scored differently. However, I can tell you based on years of experience the scoring from test to test is very similar.

ACT Goal: 24 – Top 25% in the country		
Subject	Questions correct	Percent
English	58 out of 75	77.3%
Math	36 out of 60	60.0%
Reading	29 out of 40	72.5%
Science	26 out of 40	65.0%

Much can be learned from the above table. I cover this in depth in my ACT classes, but it is important that parents understand this as well.

The ACT does not grade like high school teachers. When students look at those percents they are surprised by how low they are. At most high schools those percents would be C's, D's, and even F's at some of the private schools. When I ask students what are good percents, most respond by saying 90's and upper 80s. However, is that accurate?

If an athlete plays professional baseball and hits 40 percent (.400) they will make billions of dollars as that feat has only be accomplished once in the history of major league baseball (Ted Williams). If an athlete plays professional basketball and shoots over 50 percent behind the three point line then they are considered a great shooter. The fact is that percents are subjective based on the situation.

High school instructors teach students that high percents are required in order to be successful. And, in the high school arena, that makes sense. High school tests are based on content that has already been taught, so students should percent wise perform at a higher level. Most high school teachers provide very detailed review packages, give partial credit when grading, usually include extra credit, and will even provide re-test opportunities depending on the school district. That's not the ACT.

As mentioned before, the job of the ACT is to separate students. The test provides a score that tells colleges the following:

This student has a good chance at being successful in college.

Accept this student but reject this one.

Give this student a scholarship but give this student nothing.

Give this student $10,000 and give this student $20,000.

The ACT is very good at what they do. For decades the ACT score has been a greater predictor of college success than a high school grade point average. Therefore, the test has to grade hard. If it was easy to get most of the questions correct then the ACT could not separate students and thus would not be doing its job. More importantly, besides separating students, the test also grades like most colleges which makes sense given the fact that the test is measuring a student's ability to perform at the college level. Luke learned that the hard way.

During one of my first years of teaching I taught Calculus. One of my students, Luke, was truly brilliant. He scored a 35 on his ACT without any preparation. He went to the University of Illinois on a full-ride academic scholarship in pre-Med (he's a doctor today). During Christmas Break of his freshman year, he and I had a conversation at a high school basketball game. I asked how college was going, and he said it was eye-opening.

His first test was in an Honors Chemistry course that had 450 students. On his first test he scored a 49 percent! Luke had been a straight A student his entire life. Not only was he smart, but he studied hard. I could not believe what I was hearing. I told him that I couldn't believe he failed a test. His response:

"I didn't fail the test. I had the highest grade in class. I got an A."

I asked him if that made him feel better. He said, "No, not really." He said the entire semester was like that. His highest test grade was in the 70s. He also got an A on every test.

He had a professor that used a curved grading scale. The professor would first score the exams, put them in order from lowest to highest, and then use percents to determine how many As and Bs would be given. In other words, only 5 percent of students received an A, 10 percent got a B, and then the rest of the grades were based on the performances of the A and B students. This is very similar to how the ACT grades.

There are college professors that use the traditional model of grading similar to most high school instructors. There will also be college instructors who use a curve. Welcome to the next level of higher education.

Each test grades differently. Looking back at the previous chart notice that all the percents are different and yet they are all scores of 24. English grades the hardest which makes sense since 40 of the 75 questions are grade school concepts (this is covered in my ACT classes). Math grades the easiest. Our country is not strong in math compared to other advanced countries around the world. Reading and Science can easily fluctuate because there are only 40 question on each test.

Be prepared to miss. From a test taking standpoint, the most important numbers are the following: to earn a 24 a student can miss 17 on the English test, 24 on Math, 11 on Reading, and 14 on Science. I actually know students who honestly thought they would get a perfect score on the ACT without any preparation. Unfortunately, they "learned" this in high school from their teachers because they were used to getting 100 percent on all their tests in school. Then they took the ACT, came to a question they didn't know, and they panicked because they had never experienced that feeling before.

Students need to learn how to execute a "clean" test. It's okay to miss questions; one just doesn't want to miss questions they should get correct. This is where knowing the number of acceptable misses can help. If a student can miss 17 on the English test and comes to a question they don't know, then that will be one of the 17 questions the student misses. Knowing this helps the student relax during the test. Controlling one's emotions is so important on the ACT.

This is a test-taking strategy that will help a student throughout college and serves as an example of how the ACT is a strong predictor of college success.

Know your goal. I encourage students to take the test early. Scores do not lie. The first set of test scores will give the student – and more importantly the parents - a better idea of where the student is ranked compared to the rest of the country.

I also tell my students to be happy with their first set of scores. This does not mean they have to be satisfied with them. Too often students across the country wait until April of their junior year to take their first ACT only to find out a few weeks later where they are at nationally. Unfortunately, many students are disappointed and now must play catch-up.

How early is too early? My daughter took her first ACT in June right after seventh grade. That same year I had an eighth grader in my spring ACT classes who took her first ACT that April and scored a 28! At the time of this writing, I have had over fifty middle school students attend my ACT classes and take their first ACT before entering high school. I understand that many reading this book have students already in high school, so a more realistic timeline will be explained.

Some test dates are better than others.

The following chart outlines the basic annual timeline of the ACT.

ACT Test Dates	
Test Date	**Registration Deadline**
September.......................................middle of August	
October...middle of September	
December.......................................early November	
February...middle of January	
April...early March	
June...early May	

Register online at www.ACTstudent.org.

I cannot emphasize enough the importance of starting the ACT process early; therefore, I will not. Instead I will let Jim tell you via a letter he sent me. Jim took my summer ACT classes between his sophomore and junior years of high school.

Jim's Letter

I had several reasons for taking your summer course. I wanted to get a head start on preparing for this very important test. My sister took your class and told me that it really helped her. I, looking for a rewarding and constructive summer activity, listened to her advice and signed up for the class.

Many people are misinformed about the ACT and form unrealistic or arbitrary goals about what they want their results to look like. I, however, do not fall into that category. I understand that an ACT score in the high 20's is very pivotal to my future plans.

I have had the desire to attend the University of Illinois for a very long time. Understanding the importance of the ACT for acceptance at the U of I, I wanted to do everything within my power to achieve a good score. That was the primary reason for taking your summer class. Initially, your class didn't pay quite the dividends that I expected. That was my fault. I was overwhelmed by the ACT. At my high school, we don't cover any ACT material until the 11th grade. I was completely ignorant when it came to the ACT. I was intimidated by all of those bright kids who were in their comfort zones, already knowing what they were doing. They would always do so well on those practice tests you gave out; meanwhile, I was terribly confused.

I listened to most of the things you said. I read for usually 2 hours a day, I really wanted to do well, and I signed up for the September test. Leading up to the September test, I began feeling some anxiety. In response, I basically stopped studying and prayed that my natural abilities would take over come test day. I didn't take the ACT on September; it took me.

A couple of weeks later, I came home from school and got the news from my mother that I got a 20! I was demoralized and embarrassed. I knew that that score didn't accurately represent my abilities. I ended up having to shrug it off and pretend like it never happened.

Unfortunately, I told my English teacher about you and my September test and my plans to improve my score. She told me that I was making too big of a deal about the ACT. She thought it was foolish to take the ACT early and often and told me that it was improbable to change my score by that much. With the exception of Emma (a Christmas Break student of yours who took the February test), no one in my school took the ACT before the PSAE. My peers and teachers found out about me taking the ACT early and they were thoroughly confused. The concept of taking the ACT a couple of times before the PSAE was completely foreign to them. They thought I was crazy.

It was November, basketball had just started and our school musical was coming up. I was very busy and this helped me keep the ACT out of my mind. The December ACT kept on approaching. Around Christmas time I found out that I score a 25 on it.

I was very happy with my score. I knew I needed to improve it by a few points. My oldest brother scored a 27 and my sister got a 26. Both were accepted into the General LAS program at U of I. I wanted to beat both of them and get accepted into the very same program.

With basketball season in full swing during January and February, I put the ACT thing to rest for a little bit. In mid-March I started studying a lot. I memorized all of the Math formulas and shortcuts. I went over my English rules. Your information about the Reading and Science tests really helped me. Basically, I sucked it up and learned how to comprehend those passages. Your strategies on looking for key words and really analyzing the graphs helped me tremendously. The National April ACT came and I was in the zone. Everything went perfectly.

The PSAE ACT was a very interesting day. That morning I found out that I got a 28 on the National April ACT! I was filled with excitement from my good news. I was in the school's gymnasium. All of my classmates were in there with me. We took the PSAE ACT. Most all of my classmates didn't feel like the day went well. The whole day was a complete circus.

It is funny. The people who thought I was crazy for taking the ACT four times are now jealous of the fact that I have a 28 under my belt. They are anxiously awaiting their PSAE ACT results and are preparing for the June test. I do not care if those scores ever come back and I am thrilled that I do not have to worry about the ACT any longer. I want to thank you, Mr. Franklin, for introducing me to the ACT. I strongly believe that all students should take your class the summer before they become juniors.

Learn from Jim's classmates. Jim's classmates thought he was crazy for taking a summer ACT class before his junior year. Jim's teachers discouraged him from taking the test early and often. And yet when April rolled around, Jim was the one who was prepared, not his classmates. Jim's classmates didn't do anything extra to prepare and paid a price. The ACT is an international competition against the best students in the world; students need to do extra to get ahead.

The Ideal ACT Long-Term Plan

Step #1: Take the ACT in June

Your student should take the ACT in June right after the end of their sophomore year. The ACT allows a student to buy back a copy of the June ACT and the student's answers. The ACT only offers this service for the National June, December, and April ACT tests. This is invaluable.

1. Colleges don't care how many times a student takes the ACT; they just want to know what the student's highest ACT score is.

2. The student will learn what the test feels like.

3. This is most important - the student can learn what to specifically focus on by reviewing their actual results.

Step #2: Take the Summer ACT Classes

Summer is an ideal time to prepare because there is no school day to worry about. Students can focus on the ACT and learn how to be a better test performer without the many distractions that come during the school year. After one of my summer classes was completed, a father called and said,

"I am so thankful our son took your summer classes. You got him motivated about college. He started talking about his future and what he wanted to study. He changed his habits and we could see that your class helped him mature. He was ready for high school when it started up. Thank you."

Research shows that the better a student does on the ACT, the better they will do in college. The ACT reveals what a student needs to work on. The ACT is not testing how well a student did in high school, but rather is the student ready for college. Knowing how to prepare for the ACT is really learning how to prepare for college. This goes back to why it is so important to start early.

As an example, many of my summer students quickly learn they don't read enough and what little they read tends to be the wrong type of material. However, it is summer so they have more time to read. I provide them with a suggested reading list, explain each item on the list, and give them two specific books to start with during the summer. At this point they are just over two years from starting college but already working on the most important academic skill that leads to college success: reading comprehension. This leads not only to a higher ACT score, but greater success in high school and eventually college. It's a win all the way around.

I have other students that realize they have math deficiencies from their previous two years of high school. They now understand that simply taking a high school math course is not enough for them; they need to do additional work outside of the school day. Some realize they need a tutor. Others enroll in an evening community college course to strengthen those skills.

In the previous two paragraphs these students understood that more needed to be done and fortunately had the time to do it. This is why students need to take the test and prepare early. The longer a student delays this process, the less time they have to work on areas of weakness.

Step #3 (optional): Take the September or October ACT
The point of the summer class is to teach students how to be a better test performer not only for the ACT but on high school exams as well,

especially since the junior year is much more challenging than the sophomore year. Many summer students are motivated after the class is completed and will want to take the September or October ACT because they want to see how much they improved. Encourage this.

Step #4: Take the December ACT

The December ACT allows you to buy back a copy of the test and student's answers just like the June ACT. Again, this allows the student to see their specific mistakes, so they have a better idea of what to focus on next time. This also allows students to compare their June and December answers. Were the same mistakes made? What areas showed improvement? My ACT classes teach students how to self-assess which in turn leads to long-term success.

Step #5: Spring Semester Focus

At this point the student has taken the ACT two or three times going into January of their junior year. This gives the student a better idea of what they need to focus on during the spring of their junior year in order to get ready for the April ACT. This puts the student way ahead of most juniors who they will be competing with on the April ACT exam.

Step #6: Take the April ACT

The student is now prepared and should take the April ACT with confidence.

> ## Long-Term Plan Alternative: June ACT Test Prep Crash Course
> Some students do not feel comfortable taking the June ACT test without any preparation. In recent years, more and more sophomores have taken my June ACT Test Prep Crash Course prior to the June ACT test date. Some choose to do this because their summer schedules are so busy they just do not have time to take the summer class. This has been a successful alternative.

I mentioned earlier that my daughter took her first ACT in June right after her seventh grade year. I had her take my June ACT Test Prep Crash Course in order to make sure she had a strong feel for the test. I was very concerned that she would be intimidated walking into a test center surrounded by students so much older. It really helped her. She was very confident and felt prepared.

My daughter took it for the second time in December of her eighth grade year. Her composite score improved three points and again tested at the college readiness level in multiple subjects. More importantly, she said she was much more confident in part because she knew what to expect when she walked into the testing center since she already had previously taken the test.

For those that do not live in Central Illinois, I have an online video class that allows students to receive the same type of preparation that I provide in my live classes. The online video class can start whenever the student is ready and be used wherever the student has internet access.

*I have worked with over 10,000 students and those that start preparing prior to their junior year tend to do better when it counts:
the April ACT test of junior year.*

Students that have test anxiety tend to shy away from taking tests. This is the wrong approach. Students who know they struggle taking tests often need to take the ACT more often in order to practice.

Emily was a nervous wreck when it came to tests. She took her first ACT and scored a 22. She was not happy with her score, told me she was not a good test taker, and asked me what she should do. I told her to take it again. The next time she scored a 23. Again, she was not happy, told me she was not a good test taker, and asked me what she should do. I told her to take it again. She did and scored a 24. We went through this same scenario two more times and she scored a 25 and 26, respectively.

Emily was thrilled with her 26! Her five ACT test dates were September, December, February, April, and June of her junior year of high school. She took my ACT prep class the summer before her September test, so her ACT journey was approximately 12 months. It was a joy to watch her overcome her test anxiety, learn how to control her emotions, deciding to no longer allow tests to control her, and achieve a great score. She earned a higher score, but more importantly she better prepared herself for the challenges she would face in college.

Chapter 9

Scholarships

Scholarships, scholarships, scholarships!!! Many parents want to know how to get scholarships. Many submitted questions deal with scholarships. The following questions address many of the concerns of those questions submitted.

Can you provide advice on getting scholarships and being able to get the most amount of financial aid?

I included this parent concern in order to set-up a framework for families.

Politics matter. That's the reality. Unfortunately, politics have a lot to do with financial aid because political leaders make decisions that can affect the economy at the national and state level. At the time of this writing, we are in a recession despite what national leaders attempt to say. The reported unemployment is almost 8 percent; however, the real unemployment rate (includes people who have given up looking for work or underemployed) is over 15 percent.

Many unemployed adults have returned to college. Many of these people qualify for financial aid, many families qualify for financial aid, college costs go up every year, so the last few years there has not been enough funds to support all the students that qualify. In short, do not think you are going to get help from the government. If you do, you lose. The government has a history of not managing money well.

During the summer of 2013 Congress and the president were debating what the interest rates should be on student loans. Student loan interest rates were temporarily lowered due to the Great Recession. However, the federal government loses money due to the reduced rates, so rates are expected to go up in the near future. These new rates will have a major impact on students across the country. Again, do not put your hopes in our government. It literally is not worth it!

Illinois is winning? Right now, my home state Illinois is in a race with California to see which state is going to go bankrupt first…and we are winning! Our state government owes an immense amount of money to a lot of people and organizations including our public universities. Because our state economy is weak, public universities are not receiving as much funds from the private sector. In short, many of our public universities do not have much to give in regard to merit-based (determined by overall student record, not financial need) scholarships. The University of Illinois gives almost no academic scholarships and Illinois State University is beginning to have issues as well. These are just two examples. Many more could be included.

Every state is different. Do not assume that it is more expensive to attend an out-of-state school. One of my former ACT students from Peoria Notre Dame High School wanted to study engineering at the University of Illinois. She scored a 33 on her ACT. The U of I offered her no scholarship. She went to the University of Alabama where she was offered a full-ride academic scholarship.

Some public school universities need out-of-state students in order to meet their enrollment totals. Again, Illinois is different due to the fact that we have Chicago, St. Louis, and Indianapolis forming a triangle where the vast area is in Illinois. Then we have 100,000+ population hubs in Peoria, Bloomington-Normal, Champaign-Urbana, Springfield, and Decatur. In short, we have enough high school students in Illinois to fill our colleges and universities. This decreases the incentive for Illinois schools to offer attractive scholarships to out-of-state students.

Schools in Iowa, Missouri, Wisconsin, Indiana, the Dakotas, and now Michigan (thanks to the recession and a dramatically falling state population) are some of the states that rely on out-of-state students; therefore, many schools in those states offer extra incentives to out-of-state students to come.

Stacey did everything right in regard to preparing for the ACT. She first participated in my ACT prep class as a sophomore and took her first ACT in April of that year earning a 24. She took my ACT prep class again as a junior and then scored a 26 on the December ACT, a 27 on the February ACT, and then a 29 on the April ACT. She decided to do my summer ACT prep class prior to her senior year and then jumped her ACT composite to a 31 on the September ACT. She was excited!

Her grade point average was 4.87 on a 5.0 scale. She was ranked 67th out of 209 students in her graduating class. She applied early to all of the schools on her list and received honors college invitations and acceptance letters within two weeks. Before Thanksgiving of her senior year, she was offered the following scholarships:

- **Michigan State University** $15,000 per year
- **Indiana University** $10,000 per year
- **Iowa State University** $17,000 per year

Stacey was also interested in studying abroad, so Michigan State University added an additional one-time scholarship for $5,000 to the $15,000 original offer to be applied during the school year she would study overseas. Stacey is from Central Illinois and lives less than ten miles from the University of Illinois. Even though she would be an out-of-state student, it did not keep those three schools mentioned from offering her great scholarship packages.

Keep in mind that those offers are per year. If Stacey maintains a solid grade point average in college, she automatically will receive those scholarships each year. Assuming she does study abroad, her actual scholarship packages would be the following:

- **Michigan State University** $65,000
- **Indiana University** $40,000
- **Iowa State University** $68,000

EMAIL: Lisa received a big scholarship from an out of state school

Hey! This is Lisa from your fall class at Wesleyan. I'm doing exactly what you told me to do, making Oklahoma proud. I'll be attending Oklahoma State in the fall with an academic scholarship and I am more than excited. I'm majoring in Biology to become a PA. Thank you so much for all of your help! Without your class I would not be where I am today. I recommend it to everyone!

Lisa's scholarship package was $28,000 per year. Her ACT scores were 19 before the class and then a 24 after the class.

Every school is different. Scholarship packages can vary dramatically from school to school. Indiana University typically starts scholarship offerings at a 26 ACT. Northern Illinois University recently started scholarships at 22. The key is to start talking to the Admissions Office right away to find out what the criteria is for their scholarships, what does it take to move up to a higher level, etc.

Should my student apply for early decision?

The early decision concept is one of the biggest scams the college world ever came up with. In the late 90s it was exposed for what it was. In short, early decision forces top students to make an early commitment to the first school they apply to. This then allows universities to promote how many top students they have obtained. However, there is a catch. Once you decide to go to a school, then the school has no incentive to increase one's scholarship package. The student is already coming.

If the student clearly knows where they want to attend and money is not an issue then early decision makes sense. I've worked with over 10,000 high school students throughout my career; very few have fallen into that category.

Whether you pick your school in September or May, you still don't start college until the following fall. Too many students just want to make a decision in order to be done with it. Then there is peer pressure as other seniors start announcing where they will be going. This is a big decision and requires patience. There are advantages to waiting.

I had a student who really wanted to go to the University of Illinois. She had great grades and a 29 on her ACT. Her back-up school was Illinois State University. Neither school offered her an academic scholarship. ISU was the cheaper choice. She was a very shy young lady, so her individual visits (discussed later in the book) probably did not provide her an advantage. Her parents could help only a little with the cost, so the decision would strictly be financial. She kept waiting and waiting.

She contacted me the first week in April asking for advice. I encouraged her to contact both schools and ask for some type of scholarship. Initially, both schools said they had nothing to offer. She waited a little longer. She contacted me the last week of April and told me should would be going to ISU because it was cheaper. A week later she contacts me to let me know that the U of I had just called her (May of her senior year) and gave her a one year tuition free scholarship. That was enough for her to reverse her decision and attend her dream school, the U of I.

I had another student who had decided to go to Illinois Wesleyan University. She contacted me in the beginning of March to let me know she was picking IWU. I told her to let them know she really wanted to come but was not sure if she could afford it (her family did not qualify for any need – colleges know that FAFSA does not really measure what a family can truly afford). Three weeks later they increased her scholarship package $4,000. She made thousands of dollars just because she was patient.

The family in the story I just mentioned technically could afford to send their daughter to IWU by utilizing student loans. However, this family was very financially responsible and did not believe large student loans were practical. They made this very clear to their daughter: the family would contribute only so much to her education and she would need to cover the rest through savings, work, and loans.

What is the scholarship potential for out-of-state students?

This varies from school to school and state to state. The key is to ask the admissions office at potential schools. Don't be shy. They will be honest.

EMAIL: Vicky receives an out-of-state full-tuition scholarship

Jason, I took your fall ACT prep class at Peoria Christian High School. In the future (this fall) I will be attending St. Ambrose University in Davenport, IA. They have awarded me a full-tuition scholarship that has the requirements of a 4.0 GPA and a 30 or higher on the ACT to even apply for it. At St. Ambrose I will be majoring in nursing and have been pre-approved into their program. I picked St. Ambrose because it's small but still a school where I will meet new people and be able to live on campus, etc. Thanks for the class! Sincerely, Vicky

What/where is the best place to find available scholarships?

The internet is a wonderful thing. There is so much information. There are a lot of websites with scholarship information. However, many families think they can just pay for a service that is going to magically find scholarships that ideally suit their student. Seriously? There are a lot of scholarships; however, the reality is that the vast majority of scholarship funds are located right in the colleges and universities. Your focus should be there. Ask the schools for more money. Ask the schools how to earn more scholarships from them.

I have had two different people contact me who attended recent parent seminars. One was a mom, her son's top choice was an Illinois school, she asked for more money, and they increased his scholarship package $2,000 per year which totals $8,000.

The other person was a student from my ACT classes who also attended my parent seminar with his parents. His top choice is a private university in Indiana. He got a nice academic scholarship from the school, but he would still need to get an unsubsidized loan. He went back to the school, met with the admissions office, explained his situation, and they decided to increase his scholarship, so he would not need to take out the unsubsidized loan.

EMAIL: Asking leads to $8,000 thanks to parent seminar

Hey Jason,

I have decided to go to Rose-Hulman! When I visited on Friday they gave me an extra scholarship for $2,000 a year which is huge for me because it takes care of all of the unsubsidized loans I would have had to take. Thank you so much, because without your seminar I would not have known to go ask for more money! I also would not have been able to get the ACT score that allowed me to get that scholarship! I really appreciate your help and your prayers! I recommend your class to everyone I talk to who is looking toward the ACT.

I also decided to participate in Rose-Hulman's Fast Track Calculus program, which will allow me to take all of freshman Calculus in five weeks this summer. I am still waiting to hear back on whether I was accepted into it (they have a limited number of spots), but they said that if I have the desire and the aptitude to participate then I will probably get in. It will definitely be intense and challenging, but I am excited for it.

Thank you for everything!
Andy

In both examples neither family qualified for financial aid. Their scholarships were based on two important factors: the student had a strong academic record to begin with and someone was willing to ask for more money.

Again, don't be afraid to ask for more money. What's the worst thing the college could say? "No" and that's it.

Best sites to go for scholarship applications?

There are a lot of sources; however, I have never had any students or families share a truly positive experience with any particular website. I think this has to do in a large part with the fact that many have learned from me that the vast majority of scholarships come directly from the colleges and universities, so, the individual college website is where the family's energy should be placed.

SCHOLARSHIP GOOGLE SEARCH

I did learn from a parent how to effectively use Google Search in order to find specific scholarships at various universities. For example, do a google search on ACT score of 28. Use the advanced search function to limit websites to .edu sites. You can also modify searches to specific states, etc.

Many colleges have scholarship calculators on their websites. For example, Arizona State University has a freshman merit scholarship estimator. Students just enter a few pieces of information such as ACT composite, GPA, and class rank and within a minute an estimate scholarship amount appears on the page.

What are the best ways to apply for scholarships and student loans to decrease the cost of college?

Most high schools provide a financial aid night for families of high school seniors where FAFSA and student loans are usually discussed. I know very little about applying for student loans because I know getting them is a lot easier now than it was in the 20th Century, which is unfortunate.

In regards to scholarships, outside sources will require applications. Scholarships from the actual universities typically do not require any application. The school simply sends you a letter informing you how much you have been awarded. Once that is received you then want to be proactive in asking the university about how the amount could possibly be increased.

Top level scholarships such as the Presidential Scholarship usually have a more extensive process which may include an interview with the scholarship committee. These typically take place in the spring of the student's senior year of high school.

Is it worth looking for local scholarships?

Many communities have various local scholarships that often have few applicants because the amount is so small. One student applied for a local bank scholarship worth $500. The only requirement was the family needed to have an account with the bank. Only three people applied. She won. The next year, she was the only one that applied, so she won it again. The only thing she had to do was fill out an application and write one essay.

I had another student who spent time looking for community scholarships and ended up winning five that ranged in value from $500 to $1,500 each. As she told me, "I made more money doing that than working a part-time job." The best source to find these scholarships is to ask your high school's guidance counseling office. Usually, information about such scholarships is sent to the local high school guidance counseling office. Also, spend time getting familiar with the high school's website guidance counseling section of your student's high school AND other area high schools. Many list local scholarship information.

EMAIL: Multiple sources total $24K per year for Diane

Jason,

I will be attending St. Louis University next fall. I was accepted into the nursing program and plan to eventually become a nurse anesthetist or practitioner. I received some generous scholarships that made going to SLU possible. Saint Louis was my number one school all along, but being a private university we all know it is not the cheapest. In the end,

I am VERY glad I spent the hours I did trying to raise my ACT score because it paid off in the end. Thank you for everything! I couldn't have gotten here without your help!

Diane

P.S. My ACT went from a 25 to a 27. As for scholarships I am receiving $14,000 in a merit scholarship, another $7,000 grant, and 3,000 from my dad's company (Nucor) for academics. Those are all per year amounts.

How can we increase the possibility of earning college scholarships?

There are three ways. First, consider schools that offer more scholarships based on your student's base academic record: ACT score, class rank, and grade point average.

Second, improve your student's academic record. If your student is going to be a senior, then the only part left that can truly be affected is the ACT score. The test is offered in September, October, and December which gives seniors ample opportunity to improve the score. Depending on your negotiating skills, you may get a school to allow you to take the ACT in February, April, and even June (after high school graduation) in order to increase a scholarship package. The key is to talk to the school directly and learn what they are willing to do. That's what Stephanie did.

Stephanie had earned a partial softball scholarship to the University of Arkansas. She was a very good student and was told that if she could earn a 27 on her ACT then they would give her an academic scholarship that would pay for the rest of her college education. That's a great incentive. Stephanie took the ACT six times and scored the following:

23, 23, 25, 25, 26, and 25. I happened to contact her mom to ask how her last ACT went. Mom told me about the 25 and that Stephanie was discouraged.

Coincidently, I happened to contact mom on the deadline date to sign up for the June ACT. I knew Stephanie. I knew little things were keeping her from the 27. I also knew she had a lot going on in her life during her most recent ACT: leg injury, prom, and in the middle of an undefeated softball season. I asked mom if Arkansas would allow Stephanie to take the June ACT. Mom immediately contacted Arkansas and they said yes.

Stephanie's mom and I strongly encouraged Stephanie to take my June ACT Test Prep Crash Course. The ACT is a performance which requires focus. By the time my class started Stephanie would be done with school, prom would be over, graduation would have already taken place, her leg would be healed, and softball would be over (I was wrong: she missed the first day because her team made it to the state championship series).

When Stephanie came to the first class, I could tell she was focused and ready. Stephanie was not only a competitor on the field but those same traits came out in the classroom. She was also relaxed with everything else behind her. After scoring a 23, 23, 25, 25, 26, and 25, this time she scored a 30!!! The following is part of an email she sent me:

> *"As soon as I began the test it was like I was a different person. I felt completely confident in my answers, and I was no longer shaky and nervous like I had been before. I am sooo thankful that you never gave up on me and pushed me to take the test*

again. You are the best and I am so blessed to have met you and have you as my teacher."

Stephanie's story proves an important point about the ACT. Just because you get the same score does not mean you cannot improve. The key is learning from each test, assessing what you need to do to go forward, knowing how to go forward, creating a plan, and then executing the plan.

If your student is going to be a junior, then emphasize that this is the most important year of high school. For most colleges, the class rank and grade point average at the end of the junior year is what will be used on the college application. The junior year also happens to be the year when students are really deciding what type of person they are going to be. Most kids get their driver's license and have a newfound sense of freedom. Life-long friendships tend to change as some start experimenting with alcohol, drugs, and sex. As a public school teacher, I saw many good kids go bad during their junior year. Just think back to your high school years and some of the people you went to school with.

The junior year also tends to be when courses get a lot harder. Most freshmen and sophomore high school classes are much easier than junior courses, which too often leads to students not learning how to handle rigorous curriculums or how to prepare for tests. The difficulty of the junior courses get compounded by the fact that many college-bound students get more involved in varsity sports, extra-curricular activities, or decide to get a part-time job.

I work with over 1,000 high school juniors every year: they are extremely busy. Because of this, grade point averages and class ranks tend to change a lot for juniors who are not maintaining their academic focus. Keep your junior on track. They may end up benefitting from those around them who are letting their studies slip.

During a student's freshmen and sophomore years, there is one basic rule that tends to be realistic at most schools: earn all As. High school should be work and the earlier a student learns this, the better. If the student does not have an A in the class, then encourage the student to go in before or after school for help. If necessary, get a tutor (you would be surprised how many top students have tutors).

If extra-curricular activities such as sports are taking up a lot of time, then eliminate the activity. I've had a lot of students share with me that demanding sport practice/competition schedules kept them from focusing on their studies in their early high school years. Then they drop the sport as a junior, that time then gets transferred to academics, and the student does better in school. Unfortunately, some non-A grades during the freshmen and sophomore years can catch up with the student.

Emily missed out on a full-ride academic scholarship because of a B she received one semester in a freshman Art class. All her grades were As except for that one B. It did not matter to the college. She got a big scholarship, but the B in Art cost her over $20,000 ($5,000 per year).

Mike got two Bs as a freshman and As in all other classes throughout his high school years. However, those Bs kept him out of the top 10 percent of his class, which kept him at a lower scholarship level at the school he attended. Those two freshmen Bs cost him $24,000 ($6,000 per year).

The third way to improve a student's chances is to spend quality time preparing your student to meet with admissions officers. These meetings can be game changers. Valerie received a $40,000 ($10,000 per year) scholarship from a private university. She had a below average grade point average and scored an 18 on her ACT. However, she had a sparkling personality and a great life story (she overcame some major long-term health issues) that she was able to convey in a meeting.

Becca scored a 13 on her first ACT, took my class, improved to a 20, and later won a $60,000 ($15,000 per year) scholarship from an out-of-state university. Why? Because she had a very rough life, was an overachiever in every sense of the word, and was able to share her story effectively with the admissions office. (A later section deals with individual visits.)

We don't qualify for most scholarships because we don't possess a financial need. Our student is gifted. I want to know how to get more dollars based on merit. Our son got $12,000 from ISU. I believe our daughter can do better.

I had two brothers in my ACT classes who were two years apart in age. They were both straight A students, both scored a 32 on the ACT, and both went to Purdue University. The first brother got a free tuition scholarship. Two years later, the family just assumed that their younger son would get the same. He was not offered a dime. Mom was shocked and called Purdue. The school apologized but explained the first son's scholarship came out of a specific fund that was no longer available due to a lack of resources.

Your son got $12,000 from ISU, your daughter may be a stronger student, but every year is different. We have an unstable national economy and for five years certain political leaders have been attacking the "rich" in this country and threatening to raise their taxes and eliminate tax loopholes at any moment. (Tax loopholes are also known as legal tax deductions created and enjoyed by the very same politicians that created them.)

These "rich" people also tend to be very generous (read Dr. Thomas Stanley's book **The Millionaire Next Door**), but when they are told the federal government "deserves" more of their hard earned money, then the "rich" alter their decisions including donating to scholarship funds. We read about big donors who pay for buildings or athletic facilities on various college campuses; however, we do not hear much about all the alumni who donate money to scholarship programs and grants in order to help young people get through school.

The bottom line is this: donations to colleges and universities are down and have been down for the past five years. Some of it is due to the poor condition of the economy, but some of it is also due to the class warfare rhetoric that is truly unprecedented in our country's history. The scholarship your son received may have come from a source that has been eliminated or very low in funds.

Most families who send students to my ACT classes or attend my seminars do not qualify for financial need. In fact, I assume that so the information you get from me in regard to scholarships is merit-based, not need based. Once your student receives a scholarship offer from a school, then I encourage you to meet with the school and ask for more money. They may say "no" but at least you know their answer. They may increase it $1,000 per year. That may not sound like much but $1,000 times four years means you just got $4,000 for asking one question. That's pretty good.

Last year, a parent who attended the seminars asked her daughter's top choice if they could help the family out by increasing the original scholarship package in order to be more competitive with other offers she had received. They increased her total package $10,000 ($2,500 per year). The key is to be honest and kind during these conversations. There is no guarantee that it will work out in your favor, but keep the following in mind:

$10,000 is a lot of money to a student, but it is "pennies" to a college.

EMAIL: Katie earns a total scholarship package of $60,000

Hi Jason Franklin!
I took your class during the summer and I just decided that next year I am going to Drake University and majoring in Pharmacy! I got a 29 on my ACT after taking it twice and ended up getting about $15,000 a year in scholarships from them! Your class really helped me prepare for the ACT so thank you so much! I feel your class helped me so much that my little sisters are taking the class this summer! Thanks again, Katie

Can an average student in a middle class family really get scholarships?

An average student would be one that has all As and Bs maybe a few Cs and an ACT composite score of 20 with a class rank between the 25 – 50% of their class. This student would have the potential to receive some scholarships from a community college.

However, if this student had a compelling life story and the ability to communicate effectively about things that an academic record cannot show, then they would have a chance at getting some scholarship help from private schools and traditional state schools like SIU, EIU, ISU,

NIU, WIU, etc. The key is selling yourself to a college on why you deserve a scholarship.

How important are grades to the process of getting scholarships?

Grades are not important in the sense that everybody who plans on going to college is expected to get good grades. As and Bs are not exceptional. Straight As are impressive as long as they are accompanied with a great ACT score. I have had straight A students in my classes who scored below 20 on the ACT. They attended schools that gave more weight to homework and participation than test performance.

I cannot tell you how many times I have heard a parent say, "My kid gets good grades, but they are a horrible test taker." The reality is that test grades are the true indicator of performance abilities and colleges understand this. This is why the ACT is so important.

I know a student who was lazy, had mostly Cs on his high school transcript, but scored a 30 on his ACT. The University of Illinois offered him a provisional acceptance, which in his case met if he got all As and Bs his senior year then they would accept him. His 30 indicated that he was intelligent, but his grades demonstrated that he was lazy. I also know a student, who was valedictorian of her graduating class of 400 students, straight As all four years, took the ACT five times, highest score was a 19, and the University of Illinois did not accept her.

Chapter 10

Creating a College List

How can a student determine if the college "feels" right and will it be a good fit?

It takes multiple visits to a college to tell if it "feels" right. There is not one perfect school, just like there is no perfect city, and no perfect job. There are a lot of great places. There are a lot of great schools. Most students end up feeling really good at about three schools. If the family does everything I am sharing in this book, then the student will eventually get the "feel" which will lead to their final college choice.

How to match the level of selectivity to student's talents and abilities, matching a school's character with the student's character?

The first part of the question was answered with another question; however, I want to discuss the second part because this is important to me. I will first give practical suggestions and then my personal perspective.

Practical: This is why visiting campuses is important but not on those special weekends when the school is inviting hundreds to thousands of students and putting on a show for students and parents. It's not a realistic view of the school. Visit a school during the week; meet with an admissions officer; ask to sit in on a class – freshmen and senior courses; request to meet with a senior and take the student out to lunch to learn their perspective about the school; walk around campus and pay careful attention to the students; request a tour of the freshmen dorm; make note of the businesses that are on or close to campus. If you see a lot of bars, that says something about the campus as well as what the university is willing to tolerate. You will learn a lot.

If you live close enough to a potential school, spend time on the campus on various days. This can be eye-opening. Visit a campus at 10 pm on a Friday night. I've done this. There are schools where you will feel safe and there are others where you see the true character of part of student body.

For many young people, college tends to reveal their true character. Moral standards will be challenged and strengthened in some, while others will display their weak moral compass and are easily influenced by those around them. Social Media has revealed the wild lifestyles of many college students and employers have used this to eliminate potential candidates. (Please make sure your student reads the previous sentence multiple times during their high school and college years.)

Personal: My family lives minutes from the University of Illinois. The U of I is known as a national party school thanks to their unofficial St. Patrick's Day which led to the death of one of my former ACT students a few years ago. Drinking and crime is an issue on the campus. This may upset some people who love the U of I; I'm sorry, but it is true. Take a moment and compare the drinking issues and crime rates of the U of I compared to other major universities. You might be unpleasantly surprised.

Having said that, the University of Illinois has a very strong academic reputation and is within 15 minutes of my home. My children are home schooled and we practice our faith daily, so I pray my daughters will have a strong moral base; one that most likely will be challenged at school but remains intact. Also, I am not giving my kids to a college to be molded by people I don't know. I'm teaching my children to be careful with the relationships they develop, do not assume their professors have high moral standards, and judge people by their actions, not just their words.

It is also important to note that there are more than 50 religious and service student organizations at the University of Illinois. This is another advantage of a large university: a student may be exposed to more, while electing to surround themselves with those of the same mindset. Students, just like older adults, choose whom they will or will not associate with.

Last year I was speaking to a mom about her high school junior. She admitted that he had no idea what he wanted to in college and really didn't seem interested in college, so she thought he needed to attend an out-of-state school to figure things out. She also shared that her older son had similar issues, went to the University of Iowa, dropped out, moved back home, and still had no direction. I did not understand her logic: it failed with her first son, so the plan was to do the same thing with her younger son? The point of this example is that some parents think once their kid goes to college somehow everything will work out. I'm sorry life does not work that way. In her case, it might have been better sending her boys to the military. As a public school teacher I saw a lot of students with no direction join the military and quickly develop into truly honorable and upstanding young people.

I've taught in small and large high schools. You can learn a lot about a small school's culture in one day. However, it would take closer to a month to learn about a large high school's culture because there are so many different groups. The same is true with college with one exception. In high school you are forced to associate with the people you attend school with. However, in college, you have the ability to choose who you associate with. In short, it's not necessarily finding a school that matches your student's character as much as your student being able to find students on any campus that have similar character.

Private Christian colleges definitely have their own culture and higher moral standards than traditional public universities. Catholic universities tend to be more conservative than most colleges and universities. Southern state schools definitely have southern hospitality throughout their campus. I have found Indiana and Kentucky schools to have very friendly campuses. However, these are generalizations based on my personal visits to college campuses as well as what families have reported back to me. The key is to visit campuses and find out for yourself what their culture is like by gaining first-hand experience.

As we have done with past topics, we will set-up a basic framework in order to deal more specifically with creating a list.

Who is paying for college?

Family: It is so important to have a family meeting to discuss this. Parents need to know how much they can contribute and then make it clear to the student. This is the maximum amount and no more.

After one of my seminars, a dad came to share a story with me to pass along to other families. He has six kids. He set money aside for a college fund before his eldest was college aged. The deal was that the fund would go to the oldest child as a no interest loan. Once the oldest child graduated from college, the loan would be paid back to the family college fund, so then that money could be used by another sibling. All of the siblings knew this was how it was supposed to work. Unfortunately, theory is not always reality.

Hanna was the first child. She went off to college and needed to use most of the college fund. Her brother Michael was three years behind her in school, so there would only be one year when they were both in school. The family thought their "plan" would still work.

When Hanna graduated from college, she could not find a job that would cover her living expenses and allow her to pay back the loan. The Great Recession of 2008 came and dad was no longer able to contribute to the family college fund like he had in the past. All of a sudden, the family college fund lost two sources of revenue: dad and Hanna's payments which totaled approximately $26,000.

Hanna then decided to marry a youth pastor and told the family last spring that she was not going to pay back the loan. I could tell the dad was grieved about this even as he was sharing this story. His third child, Doug, was finishing up his junior year of high school and the family was not sure how he would be able to afford college since the family college fund had been practically depleted. But the bigger issue can be summed up in dad's statement to me:

> *"This has created a lot of tension in my family, especially among my kids. That fact that she is not paying us back hurts and really upsets her younger brothers and sisters, because she is now negatively affecting their college decisions."*

Dave Ramsey warns people about loaning money to family members. Too often family members do not feel obligated to pay these loans back. It is unfortunate because this does destroy family relationships. Hanna is in her mid-20s and I truly wonder if she understands the pain she is causing her family. Her dad shared his story with me, so I could use it to warn other families. You have been warned.

Work: Is the student going to work during the summer and/or during the school year. How much of the earned income will go directly to paying for college? Be very realistic and conservative with this figure. We are still in a recession with signs things are going to get worse not better. Part-time jobs given to college students tend to be the first to go. Work-study programs offered at various colleges are great but also not guaranteed. I have had many former ACT students lose their work-study job or have their hours reduced due to budget cuts. Be careful when calculating this part of the budget.

Loans: Just because a student can get a loan does not necessarily mean they should maximize the loan amount. The family needs to help the student determine what an acceptable loan amount would be because it is going to have to be paid back by the student, not mom and dad. Take the time to explain to the student the total cost of the loan, the monthly payments that will begin almost immediately after college, and whether or not it is worth taking on that responsibility in five or so years. This is a great life lesson for them to have now and will help them throughout life when managing finances.

Scholarships: This part is tricky at the beginning because scholarship packages typically do not come out until after Christmas Break of the student's senior year. However, you can ask schools about their scholarship programs. Some schools have set guidelines and others school do not. It never hurts to ask. You might be surprised what you find out.

Athletic scholarships usually are given much earlier, which takes pressure off of the student-athlete. Partial athletic scholarships are very popular among the minor sports and smaller schools. If the student-athlete has a strong academic record then the college coach will have a better ability to work with the admissions office to get the student a partial academic scholarship in order to provide the student-athlete a free college education.

Location Preferences and Advantages

In-State vs. Out-of-State: The last census revealed that over half of Americans live within 50 miles of where they were born. College-bound students tend to follow the same pattern. Many high school students talk about wanting to go away to school, but most really would like to be close enough to get home easily. Going out-of-state sounds so appealing to many 17 year olds. However, the reality is that most students stay in-state for three primary reasons:

1. It usually cost less to stay in-state.

2. Most students really do prefer to be close to home just in case they need to get back quickly.

3. It is easier to visit schools and get familiar with campuses that are closer to home.

It's hard to learn about out-of-state universities without spending a lot of time and money making multiple trips to visit. For most, this is just not feasible during the busy high school years.
Families need to determine the geographical region that is reasonable. Do not let a student start looking all over the country. There are over 7,000 different types of post-secondary schools. It's not possible to investigate all of them. Focusing on specific states will help eliminate a lot of schools.

Maria was interested in Arizona State University. Her dad contacted me about ASU. My first thought was, that is far away from Central Illinois? A quick google search revealed that approximately 75 percent of ASU students are from Arizona. Maria would not have as much in common initially with three – fourths of the student body nor would she be able to visit home as frequently as other students on campus.

These concerns were shared with Maria's dad. He explained that if Maria chose to attend ASU then the family would move to Arizona. Maria was an only child and the parents were in a financial position to move. In fact, she was also looking at schools in Florida and the family was willing to move there as well.

The fact that Florida and Arizona are both attractive states for retirement was a factor in Maria's decision due in part to the fact that if Maria's parents moved to either state then Maria would eventually become an in-state resident.

City vs. Community: Approximately half of the University of Illinois students are from the Chicago area. Many think Champaign-Urbana is a nice small community. I think Champaign-Urbana is a great size and I get stressed in the City of Chicago. We all have different tolerance levels.

I have worked with a lot of small town students that think they want to go to school in a big city UNTIL they actually visit the big city. One girl who visited a private university in Chicago was shocked when she only saw concrete on the campus: few trees, very little grassy areas, etc. That's what many city schools are like.

Spend time traveling around the geographical region when visiting schools. Get to know the area. This is where your student will be living for four years. I would encourage families to take advantage of the internet and research what companies are located close to the school, crime rates, unemployment rates, local entertainment, and would I even attempt to get copies of local newspapers, preferably online. For example, one could learn a lot about the University of Illinois by reading The News-Gazette, Champaign-Urbana's daily newspaper. If you know someone from your community who attended or attends the school, talk to them about the area.

How can we find a safe school?

This is a great question and one that requires the family to use common sense because a university is not going to tell you how safe – or unsafe – they are. Illinois State University and Illinois Wesleyan University both have safe campuses primarily because they are located in one of the safest twin cities in Illinois: Bloomington – Normal. I personally would be nervous about any school located in Chicago, Washington D.C, or New York City due to the well-known crime issues. However, I have had students that attended universities in Chicago and absolutely loved the big city life. Every student (and family) needs to decide what level of location safety is acceptable.

In the bigger cities it is also important to know what neighborhoods the schools are located in. Take for instance the city of Chicago. Depaul University is on the north side of Chicago next to neighborhoods of young professionals where a student would not need to have great concern for their safety. Compare that to the University of Chicago which is in the midst of Chicago's south side, where surrounding neighborhoods are not as safe. Two schools in the same city can have different levels of safety. It is important not to rule out a school because you are concerned about what city it is in, instead visit and through visiting you will be able to get a better gauge of how safe your student will feel.

Unfortunately due to the nature of the world, women must be more cautious than men, and that is something to consider as well. Attempt to get a list of recent college graduates in your area from the particular school your student is considering. Since they are recent graduates they will be more apt to be honest about issues such as safety. It will also provide an excellent opportunity to get additional information about the school.

Work & Internship Opportunities: Most families do not think about this, but it is a very important factor to consider when selecting a college. Work and internships are what a college graduate really needs on their initial resume, not necessarily the name of the college and grade point average. Ask colleges what is available and how internships are distributed among the student body.

Consider Illinois State University and Illinois Wesleyan University. Both are located in Bloomington-Normal, IL, the national headquarters of State Farm and Country Companies. This gives those universities easy access to major internships. That is a selling point for both schools.

Big cities like Chicago, St. Louis, and Indianapolis have a lot of work and internship opportunities. For example, Butler University is near downtown Indianapolis and very close to a lot of companies.

Schools in rural areas, especially smaller universities, may have more challenges in providing internships and work opportunities. I know students that had to re-locate during the senior year of college in order to complete an internship. That would be stressful.

Certain majors are easier to obtain internships than others. The more specialized the major the more challenging the internship placement will be.

Student's Learning Style

I have lived in the Champaign-Urbana area my entire life. The community tends to center around the University of Illinois. Most high school students in the area think all colleges and universities are just like the U of I. They don't realize how unique the U of I really is compared to most other schools. However, potential schools should not be based on familiarity with an area school but rather one's learning style.

The Quiet Learner. If your student is quiet, likes to just sit in a high school and listen to the teacher, simply does the work asked, and that's it then your student may be more suited for bigger schools. Big schools tend to have very large classes (hundreds of students). These courses truly are lectures with no student participation. The first two years of college will most likely be like that at a big school.

Do not be deceived by student-faculty ratios at bigger schools. These numbers are deceptive because they include graduate courses which are very small. When visiting a bigger school, ask to see a lecture course or simply ask the admissions office how big is the biggest class on campus.

The Proactive Learner. If you have a student that likes to talk in class, debate with teachers, go in for help before or after school, then your student needs to seriously consider smaller schools, particularly private universities.

I had a student who was convinced she wanted to go to the University of Illinois. This girl loved to participate in class, was highly involved in extra-curricular activities, and could sing and dance. She just had a personality that seemed more typical of a student who would excel at a small private university. She thought I was crazy! I finally convinced her to visit Illinois Wesleyan University, since it was a smaller school and not a far drive from Champaign. (I confess. I also called her mom to help motivate the daughter.) She really liked IWU and the visit encouraged her to consider other private universities. She ended up not even applying to the U of I. She finally chose Miami University in Ohio, a school with an undergraduate enrollment around 15,000 compared to almost 32,000 at the U of I.

Keep the list small & evolving.

I had a student once tell me they were going to apply to 25 schools. That's ridiculous. I eventually talked her and her parents down to a list of ten schools, which they soon learned was still too many. The problem is applying to colleges is what a student should do after doing their research and visits. After your family has discussed the previous points, then use those parameters to determine possible schools. However, attempt to keep the list limited to five schools. This will allow your family to gather all necessary information about those particular schools. Don't add a school unless one has been eliminated from the list. This will help maintain focus.

Warnings when Creating a List

Choose the school not the major. Too many families want the decision based on what school provides the best program for a specific major. I understand why parents think this would be a good place to start; however, it's not realistic. Many studies show that the average college student changes their major three times during the first two years of college. This makes sense: 18 and 19 year olds change a lot when they leave home. They are learning about themselves and their views about life are changing. However, if a student picks school A because it has a great English program and then later switches to Business, they may not necessarily prefer the school.

MYTHS ABOUT MAJORS

The University of La Verne (California) has an excellent web page on this topic. The following is a portion of it. The entire text can be found at http://sites.laverne.edu/careers/what-can-i-do-with-my-major/.

Myth: Most students entering college have already decided their academic majors.

Reality: National statistics vary but most state that at least 50% of entering college students are undecided about their majors.

Myth: Once a student decides on an academic major, he/she will stick to it.

Reality: Not likely. 50% – 70% of students change their majors at least once, most will change majors at least 3 times before they graduate.

Myth: Student should choose a major based on current job trends.

Reality: Job market demands are constantly changing and what's hot today may not be hot tomorrow. Furthermore, estimates from various sources state that 40% – 60% of the jobs of the future have yet to be created!

Myth: Students should choose majors directly related to their careers.

Reality: The truth is that more than 50% of college graduates pursue careers that are not related to their majors. Keep in mind that most employers just want you to have a degree in something.

Myth: A career/personality assessment or career professional can tell you what to major in and what to do with your life.

Reality: Not. The purpose of these assessments is to help you clarify and understand your strengths, weaknesses and preferences so that you can make more confident decisions. A good career professional will help guide your decision making process but will not make these decisions for you.

Myth: A major will limit career options.

Reality: Not in the least! A math major can have a business related career just as a business major can be a psychologist. For most people, it's what you do in your graduate program or on the job that will dictate your career path. So getting back to the examples above, a math major can go on and get a Masters in Business Administration (MBA) and a business major can go on and get a graduate degree in Psychology.

Myth: A college degree guarantees career success.

Reality: Unfortunately, there are no guarantees. What a college degree does do however, is increase the odds that you will be gainfully employed and that if you lose your job, you will spend less time unemployed than someone without a college degree.

What can I do with a major in...?

> The truth is, you can do any job with almost any major. While some careers require you to receive specialized training to perform specific job tasks or to advance in the field, employers usually don't hire based on your major. They look for candidates who are willing to learn new skills, demonstrate strong work ethic, and are a good personality fit within their organization. They also take volunteer, internship and work experience into consideration.

College is not job training, it is mind training. Your student is going to change a lot once they leave high school. Support them, encourage them, but do not pressure them to figure out life at the age of 17 or 18 years old. Be honest, did you know what you would be doing at that age?

Broad Area of Study vs. Specialties. I recently visited with a former ACT student and asked what she was studying. The program was so detailed that I cannot even remember the complete name. I had never heard of it. It was a human development major dealing with child and family services, but she had a dream job within that field that was more specific. She saw the unusual expression on my face and explained that it was a very small field of study nationally.

Here's the problem (and I told her this as well): what happens if you cannot find a job in that field? Her major was so detailed that it gave her no flexibility. That's a problem. She really needed to start with a human development major, which would later give her the option to go into early childhood education or family and consumer sciences. That would give her more options.

Studies have shown that over 80 percent of college graduates enter a professional field that does not utilize their undergraduate degree "knowledge." I am a teacher. Most teachers will tell you the following:

"College does not prepare you for teaching."

Think about that for a moment. Most teachers do not feel that college helped them get ready to become a teacher. College is more closely associated with teaching than any other degree program!
Very specialized undergraduate programs can be a problem. Starting out in those programs can be even worse, because it makes it harder to change majors without falling too far behind in regard to credit hours. It's better to take required general education courses your first few semesters that can be applied to a broad range of majors.

I was meeting with a student who wanted to be a marine biologist. She had attended some special camps focused on marine biology and loved it. The problem is that not many schools have marine biology programs and she was having trouble locating schools based on her other parameters for selecting a college. I asked for more details about the camp. A lot of college graduates worked at the camp, so I encouraged her and her mom to find out what the workers' undergraduate degrees were. She did and learned that all of them had biology degrees, not one person had an undergraduate degree in Marine Biology.

It's perfectly acceptable to go to college undeclared and focus on completing general education requirements that tend to be necessary for most undergraduate programs. A great broad area of study is business. The reality is that the private sector is critical to our country's success and everyone should have a basic understanding of how the business world works.

There are many majors that are easier to switch out of, than transfer into. I would advise students to select the more difficult major they may be interested in (i.e. Engineering, Business, Pre-Med, Architecture, Veterinary Program). I would also advise the student to consider studying something that may be difficult to learn on one's own, and would be useful in a job post-graduation. Although they may be interested in philosophy or history, the skills learned while earning this degree are not transferrable to many occupations.

Do not be fooled by magazine college rankings. Rankings are highly subjective and are meaningless. Companies hire individuals and what one has accomplished in the real world via work and internships. Companies are not hiring the university name that ends up one's college degree.

Recently, I had a meeting with a parent and her daughter, Jane. Jane was the family's third child to go through my ACT classes. At the end of the meeting I asked Jane's mom how the other two were doing. Their oldest went to the University of Illinois, could not handle the environment, and dropped out to return home. His mom said he went from being the big fish in a small pond at his high school to a small fish in a big sea at the University of Illinois.

She and her husband reached out to the U of I in attempt to find programs to help him adjust to the big college setting. He was simply overwhelmed. The mom did not blame the University of Illinois. She knew many students who had great experiences there; it just was not the right school for her son. Four years later, he still had not recovered from his unfortunate U of I experience. This is why it is so important not to get caught up in the name of a school but rather consider what type of school will best fit your student.

Do not be swayed by college athletic programs (unless of course you plan on playing sports there). College athletics are advertising tools used by universities to recruit students. Just look at all the promotional materials you receive from colleges and universities: most include a sports picture somewhere on the advertisement. And it works!

Butler University defied the men's college basketball world when they made it all the way to the NCAA Tournament Championship game not once but twice in consecutive years: 2010 and 2011. What was the impact? Butler University received a record number of applicants. March Madness made BU famous. I even saw it in my ACT classes. Students started asking me questions about Butler.

However, unless you have athletic scholarship offers, then college sports should not be a factor in the decision. I had one student tell me they wanted to go to a college where they could attend major college sporting events. I gave him the following example. A student could attend Millikin University (Decatur, IL), Illinois Wesleyan University, Illinois State University, Heartland Community College, Richland Community College, Danville Area Community College, Eastern Illinois University, and Parkland College – all within 60 minutes of the Champaign – Urbana – and still attend University of Illinois athletic competitions.

I had another girl who wanted to attend the University of Illinois because she wanted to be in the Orange Crush – the U of I student cheering section at athletic events. At first I thought she was joking, but I soon realized she was very serious. She had already talked to members of the Orange Crush to learn more about the student group. I asked if she met with the admissions office to learn more about the school. "Nope." That's not exactly the best approach to picking a school but serves as a great example of how powerful the attraction of college sports can be when one is looking at colleges.

EMAIL: Jim provides some practical advice for younger students

Hi Jason, this is Jim and I'm graduating from Normal Community in a month! I hope all has been well and your classes are going great.

Next year I plan on attending Illinois State as I was accepted directly into BS/MPA 5 year Accounting program. I will also be a part of the Honors College and will hopefully be a recipient of one of their scholarships as I'm currently an alternate candidate.

I didn't look at very many schools during my college process because I knew ISU had a very well respected accounting program, but I would encourage future students to look at a variety of schools. This would include a large school (Big Ten), mid major type school (like ISU), a smaller school (private), and an out of state school. I believe that this allows for students to gather the complete feel of each type of school and can narrow the choice of size of the school they wish to attend very quickly.

I would also encourage students to begin looking at essay requirements and applications before they can be sent to the school. Many schools have their prompts on the website. Having an essay written for your school of choice and submitting an application as soon as it is available is essential. Applying early allows for plenty of time to decide on schools and apply for their scholarships.

I have learned this through my college process and being the oldest student in my family. I hope it helps! Thank you very much again for all your help with the ACT! - Jim

Chapter 11

Comparing Types of Schools

Many parents submitted questions that prompted the creation of this section. Questions seemed to fall into the same groups, so I have included the basic questions and my responses.

What are the advantages and disadvantages of public vs. private colleges?

I am going to re-word this question by discussing the differences because advantages and disadvantages vary depending on the individual students. Some students will excel more in a private school and others will excel more in a public school. This goes back to understanding what best suits your student.

Public: These schools have lower sticker prices, tend to be bigger, have more opportunities available however those opportunities must be spread out among a larger student body, and usually have more name recognition thanks to our country's love of college sports. The first two years of college, primarily general education courses, students will often be taught by graduate assistants or adjunct professors in much larger settings (hundreds of students in a class). Bigger public universities tend to be involved more in research which opens up opportunities for graduate students and helps bring recognition to the school.

Private: These schools often have higher sticker prices but have the ability to put together attractive scholarship packages in order to incentivize top students to attend their schools. Many of these universities have smaller populations, which leads to much more of a family atmosphere on campus allowing for an easier transition from high school to college, especially during the freshman year.

Most private schools focus on teaching over research, so students are being taught by professors every year and the class sizes are much smaller: under 50 students the first two years and usually lower than 15 the last two years depending on the major. Private schools encourage participation in extra-curricular activities and make it easy to do, particularly at Division III schools. Sports are not emphasized nor have the restrictions that most Division I powers have, so squads are larger and practice/game time during the week is limited because academics come first.

There are smaller public universities that have a private school atmosphere due to their size but are less expensive than private colleges. The University of Illinois at Springfield is a great example.

129

The major difference between a small public school and small private university would be the quality of typical student attending. Private universities tend to have very competitive students due to higher standards for acceptance. Top tier public universities like the University of Illinois in Champaign-Urbana also tend to have competitive students due to the fact that have a much higher number of students applying, allowing them to require higher ACT scores, grade point averages, and class ranks.

What is the value comparison between a public university, private university, and community college?

Community colleges are the best financial value and serve as a great way to quickly and inexpensively complete one's general education requirements. Traditional public universities like Eastern Illinois University and Indiana State University would be the next level of cost effectiveness. Private universities can be expensive or moderate depending on the quality of the student applying. There are exceptions. The University of Illinois is very expensive and Illinois State University is not far behind.

I know there are parents that feel the name of the school provides value in the job market. There is no research to support that concept. However, we all know exceptions. I worked in an e-commerce start-up when the concept of purchasing online seemed dangerous. The president of the company had an MBA from the University of Illinois. One year I served on the team that interviewed all potential job candidates.

Every candidate that had gone through the U of I MBA program was hired, even when the team did not think an offer should be given.

Because the president felt a kinship to anyone who had been through the MBA program, he hired them automatically. In this case, the name of the degree made a difference. I also need to point out that in one year we hired six executives right out of the U of I MBA program, and four of them were fired or left within one year due to lack of performance or lack of job satisfaction. Ironically, the two most valuable executives we hired were individuals in their 50s who had years of successful marketing and sales experience AND no college education.

Bigger schools do have larger networks simply because they graduate more students every year. That cannot be denied. Networks can help recent graduates find their first job. However, bigger schools also have MORE recent graduates looking for jobs as well as opposed to smaller private universities which can assist those that need additional help. The point is that there are advantages and disadvantages to all colleges and universities.

The name on your degree may help you get your first job, but for the rest of your life your employability will be based upon previous work experience which has nothing to do with a college degree.

How to find a smaller private school that is competitive yet also affordable for more modest family incomes?

Most private schools are very competitive because they have the ability to push students harder the first two years of college as opposed to big public universities that cannot push students due to extremely large class sizes. If the student has a strong academic record and strong communication skills, most private universities are able to provide scholarship packages that can make their school less than a public university. The key again is asking.

If a parent is concerned about their student finding a job after finishing a degree at a private school, the advantage can be gained by what the student does outside the classroom. How they work to develop themselves as a person through jobs, internship, taking leadership roles on teams or in organizations. This is what is going to make a person a desirable candidate for a job no matter what university they are coming from.

For a high achieving student, is it important that they start at a university despite having no strong conviction on a study plan?

Absolutely not. A high achieving student most likely has characteristics that will make them successful regardless of where they start. Most community colleges offer full-ride scholarships to top achieving students in an effort to attract stronger students. As an example, Parkland College does this. If a student was able to live at home and attend Parkland for free then transferred to the University of Illinois and graduated within two additional years, then that student just got a four-year undergraduate degree from one of the top schools in the country for half price. However, the odds are a high achieving student would be able to qualify for additional scholarships that would lower the total price even more. Not only did the student earn the degree in a cost effective manner, but also learned some valuable financial lessons along the way while starting adult life in the early 20s with little to no debt.

Recent college graduates have very little on a resume. We all know successful work experience is much more important to a corporation than a college degree. However, imagine you are supposed to hire a recent college graduate. You are down to two candidates. Both graduated from the University of Illinois and have similar academic records. One student had his college paid for by his parents. The other student started at Parkland then transferred to the University of Illinois, paying for their college with scholarships and working part-time. Her parents did not need to contribute one dime. Given the above, who would you hire?

Is the community college in our district capable of providing the curriculum she would receive at a four-year university?

A better question might be is a four-year university able to provide the instruction equivalent to what a student would receive from a community college. Talk to U of I students and ask how many people are in their general education classes. The number is in the hundreds for many classes (in some cases, over 600 students). It's very common to find U of I students taking night and/or summer classes at Parkland College (community college located a few miles from U of I) in order to save money.

The reality is most general education curriculums are the same and content learned in those courses tends to be basic introductions to different concepts to help students figure out what the student would like to study. Because these courses are general, they can be well taught by many people – not necessarily university professors - so why not save money by taking advantage of the local community college.

We are strongly interested in alternative programs to traditional college. Suggestions?

21st Century technology has changed the world and shown us that we don't know what the future holds. Advanced technology has opened up a lot of non-traditional ways to earn a college education. Online classes, webinars, and reading books written by various leaders are among some of the things that are dramatically decreasing the financial value of a traditional college education.

A traditional college education was never designed to prepare students for future employment. Those that work in the real world know this. Companies hire talented individuals and then train them for specific positions. It's been this way since before our country officially became a nation. This is why over 80 percent of college graduates don't use their major in their professional lives.

Recent reports have also shown that students who graduate from community colleges with specific certifications actually make more money that those with undergraduate degrees in "less than needed" fields. There is one good rule to follow: college and universities are at least one decade behind the private sector. All students need to be doing their own research on how to prepare themselves for the future, because most colleges are preparing you for the past.

Chapter 12

Objective Measures

The goal of every college admissions office is to select students they believe will come and graduate in four years. Many tools are used to determine which students will truly be successful. This section focuses on the objective measures.

Comparing Students throughout the Country AND World

Everyone wants to come to the United States and attend our colleges and universities. According to the CollegeNavigator.org website, approximately 13 percent of the fall 2012 undergraduate students at the University of Illinois were from other countries. Your student needs to remember that they are competing against the world, literally.

ACT (or SAT) Score: National Comparison. As mentioned earlier, the ACT is a fair test and allows schools to objectively compare students all over the state, country, and world. This test is given in over 100 different countries. This test is a big deal. Do not take it lightly.

SAT Subject Tests: National Comparison in Specific Areas. These are relatively new and not required by all schools, but top tier schools may *strongly recommend* students take some of these. They are one hour tests and a student studies for them just like a high school test. The major difference is that the grading is based on national standards and comparisons similar to the ACT and not like typical high school teachers.

On a given Saturday, a student can take one, two, or three tests. Some colleges will even allow students to combine SAT subject scores to make an equivalent SAT comprehensive score. Students pick what the test will cover. The following are the subjects a student can choose from:

Literature	*French with*	*Italian*
U.S. History	*Listening*	*Latin*
World History	*German*	*Chinese with*
Math Level 1	*German with*	*Listening*
Math Level 2	*Listening*	*Japanese with*
Biology/EM	*Spanish*	*Listening*
Chemistry	*Spanish with*	*Korean with*
Physics	*Listening*	*Listening*
French	*Modern Hebrew*	

High School Class Rank: Local Comparison. One cannot really compare the top ten percent of students at Centennial High School to

Richwoods High School or Bloomington High School. Schools are different, teachers are different, grading systems are different, and curriculums are different. However, class ranks are important because they compare a student to everyone in their class who was in the exact same environment.

Most schools then look for a correlation between the high school class rank and ACT national percentile rank. If your student's class rank is in the top ten percent, then the ACT score needs to be a 28 or higher. If not, then a red flag goes up.

One of my former students is now a teacher in an inner city school in a southern state. She contacted me for advice on how to help her school improve their overall ACT scores. She sent me the previous year's statistics. The valedictorian scored a 12 on the ACT. Not one student in the top twenty students (and this was a large high school) scored higher than a 20. These students had great grades and class ranks but did not have an ACT score to back up them up. In short, despite what they were being told by the high school, they were not ready for college and would have major trouble gaining acceptance and succeeding at most schools.

High school GPA: individual class performance. Understand the meaning behind this next point: your student's grades do not matter. Everyone going to college is expected to earn good grades. Take a moment and examine your student's high school's latest honor roll. What percent of the students made the honor roll? Most schools have over half their students on those lists. At smaller schools it reaches as high as 80 percent. The No Child Left Behind Act encourages schools to give out high grades. It's truly unfortunate. This leads to the next very important point: Cs are red flags and Ds and Fs are even worse.

The following is an example of how many students make the honor roll. I did a google search for first quarter honor roll in Illinois in the fall of 2013. I picked a small school and a big school. The following were the first two schools I found (name of schools are not included because that is not important).

Small School
181 total high school students
ACT composite average: 19.7
65.7 percent of the students made the honor roll

Big School
2,107 total high school students
ACT composite average: 23.6
48.9 percent of the students made the honor roll

Was the big school a lesser school? Quite the contrary. The big school had a much higher ACT composite average (23.6 compared to the small school's 19.7). The small school offered no AP classes, while the big school has been consistently ranked in the top 10 percent in the country based on AP test performance.

Here is the point: the big school challenged their students. Students had to work for As and Bs. More rigorous classes were offered at the bigger school, which in the long run prepared their student body more effectively for college. Less students made the honor roll, but that is not going to matter when those students reach college. They will be ready for the next level. I am not as confident that the small school students will be as well prepared for college.

We've all heard the following: it's better to be in a hard class and work to get a C than be in an easy class and be given an A. From a learning and growth standpoint that is certainly true without a doubt. However, view it from the college's perspective. How would they know your student worked hard to get the C? How would they know an A was easy? Colleges are not calling teachers asking if they grade easy or hard. Honestly, what teacher is going to readily admit they are easy?

Because As and Bs are much easier to come by in the 21st Century, colleges expect them. Therefore, when a C shows up on a high school transcript, that is a red flag. If that is your student's situation, then they need to be ready to explain the C to a college and this will need to be done before applying to a college (this is explained in a later section).

This next part is specifically written to students. Avoid getting Cs while there is still time. If you know you are border line between an A and B or a B and a C, talk to the teacher privately about your classroom performance. Ask for ways to improve the grade. Ask for extra credit. Make arrangements to come in before or after school for help. Most people become teachers because they truly want to help students.

PARENTS, DO NOT DO THIS: When I was a young teacher working in a small school district, I had a mom come talk to me about her daughter's performance. Liz was not doing well. In fact, she had the lowest percent in all my sections by at least 10 percent. She had a low D on the school's grading scale. I thought Liz's mom wanted to discuss what Liz needed to do in the last few weeks of school to potentially earn a C for the spring semester. I was wrong!

Liz's mom informed me that Liz was, and had always been, a straight A student her entire life. Liz was going to be a doctor; she could not afford to have a D on her high school transcript. Therefore, Liz's mom was requesting I change her D to an A. Let me be clear: Liz's mom was not asking for additional work or extra credit. She simply wanted me to change her grade. I was shocked and quite intimidated by the mom.

I was really bothered by the request, so later in the day I brought up the incident at a faculty meeting because I was not sure how best to handle the situation. Immediately, one teacher shared that the year before she had a similar incident with the same mom, except Liz had a B. Then another teacher spoke up and said the same thing happened to her the year before. Again, Liz had a B. Another and another teacher spoke up sharing similar stories. By the end, we discovered that Liz had straight Bs the year before, so Liz's mom met with each teacher and requested a grade change to an A since Liz was going to be a doctor.

Liz's mom was clever. She concluded each meeting with those teachers by saying:

> *"Liz does not know I am meeting with you. This is a little embarrassing. I would ask that you would not tell anyone about this meeting."*

It worked. Each of those teachers did change Liz's grade from a B to an A. Unfortunately, Liz's mom's trick was discovered and that family was watched careful by the administration during Liz's remaining time in high school.

By the way, Liz did not become a doctor.

Liz's story is extreme, I know. Unfortunately, she is not the only parent that had done that to me during my years as a public school teacher. David missed 17 days in my Calculus class including every test and

you are borderline between grades, then it is time to go talk to the teacher even if it is only a few weeks into the class. Do it as soon as possible.

The above dealt with high school performance, which allows schools to compare students based on primarily the first three years of high school. The next section deals with college level work done during the high school years.

College Level Work

AP Classes: Most students do not understand the AP program, so let me provide a very simple history lesson. AP exams were designed to provide exceptional high school students an opportunity to take a test that would be the equivalent of a lower level college course. A high score on an AP exam can lead to automatic college credit. This saves time and money in the long run.

As time went on and the AP exams became more popular, top high schools began introducing AP classes to assist students. This idea soon spread to other high schools across the country. AP class offerings soon became a selling point on the strength of a high school. Parents began demanding more AP class offerings.

High schools responded. Courses were added or names changed to reflect "AP status." Students were strongly encouraged to take AP classes because they "look good" to a college. Parents were told AP classes are more challenging and will better prepare students for college. And this is where we run into problems: marketing vs. reality.

The top two public high schools in Illinois based on ACT scores, SAT scores, AP scores, and national merit scholars are the Illinois Math & Science Academy (IMSA) and Urbana University High School on the campus of the University of Illinois. Neither school offers AP classes, and yet most of their students take AP exams and score high.

It's not the AP class that is important; it's the AP test score which measures the student's knowledge of the respective subject.

If your student takes an AP class and does not take the AP test or scores low, then that is a red flag to a university. Colleges know that many high schools simply changed course names to appease parents. For example, Biology 2 was changed to AP Biology. The teacher did not change, the curriculum did not change, only the name changed. Yes, this happened in the past and still happens today. It's unfortunate because it's the student that gets hurt in the end. Colleges do not assume just because a student is in an AP class that they are truly doing college level work. If the AP score is low or the student did not take the test, then many colleges will assume the AP class – at least for the student – was not AP level.

Is there value in an AP class? Absolutely, assuming it is an effective AP course. Therefore, families need to do some research on determining whether or not an AP class offered at the high school is advantageous. The following guidelines will help.

How many students took the AP exam last year for a given subject?
There were two teachers who both taught AP Calculus in the same school district. Out of the students that took the exam, most scored 4s and 5s in both classrooms. However, less than half of the students of one teacher took the exam while the other teacher had over 95 percent

of his students taking the exam.   As a rule of thumb, over 80% of the students should be taking the exam. After all, that is the point of the class. If the percent is less, then there may be an issue. It may not truly be an AP level course.

What were the scores on last year's AP tests? These tests are not like the ACT. They are not a secret. Schools should have copies of past exams in order to prepare for upcoming tests. Again, as a rule of thumb, over 80 percent of students taking the exam should score a 4 or 5. If the percent is less, then there may be an issue. Again, it may not truly be an AP level course.

It takes a special instructor to teach an AP class. I've worked with some great ones who annually had the previously mentioned percents over 90%. I worked with one teacher who could almost guarantee that if a student got at least a D in his class then they would score at least a 4 on the exam and every year it would nearly happen. It was truly amazing to watch.

A high AP score will trump a low grade in an AP class. Again, it is the score that is important, not the class. Great AP instructors will have students earn a C in the class but score 4 or 5 on the AP exam. This is a sign of a great teacher as well as students who were willing to work hard for an "average" grade and earned the great AP score in the end.

It's hard to find these types of teachers. They truly are a special breed. Unfortunately, high schools are not going to cancel an AP class if they cannot find a worthy instructor.

I had a family of a sophomore attend one of my parent seminars and heard the above. Before the start of his son's junior year he contacted the high school to get the above statistics. They kept promising to get back to him with the results but never did. Finally, he went to the principal who apparently was aware of the request. The principal finally admitted that most kids at the high school usually do not take the AP exam and those that have in the past did not score very high.

One, it is truly sad that the school was not providing the statistics immediately. Two, apparently the school did not really care about their AP performances because they were making no effort to improve those courses. This is what you have to watch out for.

One of my students was signed up to take an AP History class in the fall. During the summer she emailed her upcoming AP instructor the previously mentioned questions. The following was his email response.

> *"No clue...I really don't follow numbers BUT I think 3-5 out of 18 took it...I don't know scores....last year (two years ago) I think 3 people took it and 2 got a 4 or better BUT I am not really sure if that is correct. Please understand the U.S. History test is the HARDEST of the AP test...at least that is what I have been told."*

An AP History test is hard when the instructor does not track the class's test results and has no idea how to prepare students effectively.

The following is an email I received from a mom who attended my seminar and immediately spoke to the AP chemistry instructor at her son's high school (I have removed the teacher's name and high school name).

Jason,

I spoke with the instructor who teaches the AP Chem. He has taught it at *our school* for many (can't remember how many - significantly more than 5) years and at *another school* for 6 years prior to *our school*. He teaches to pass the AP Chem test. He has spent the summer revising the curriculum to meet the new test for this year.

Last school year (2012-2013), 32 students took his class. This is the most students ever to take his class. He felt that some shouldn't have taken the class. 100% took the test. 4 scored 5, 0 scored 4, 15 scored 3, 6 scored 2, and 7 scored 1. This is less than your recommended 80/80 for scoring. He noted that he felt students scoring 3's at most universities will be given a semester's worth of chemistry credit.

He believes the AP Chem test is the hardest of all AP tests and 3's are widely accepted as accomplishing the material. He felt there were students at (school name) who did not have intentions to gain the college credit, only wanted the AP class for the weighted grade or took the class to give them a good foundation for their college chem classes.

He also noted there are many students who are A students who study for a test to pass the test, but do not study to retain or apply information. There are many students who do well in their homework (share homework/copy homework/verify their answers with other students) but then do not test well. The homework helps their grade, but is not a reflection of what they understand/have learned. He noted to succeed, time studying and preparing would be (as should be) necessary. He noted many juniors are not prepared for this commitment or have not developed the study habits needed to succeed in the class.

He also teaches a dual credit Honors Chemistry II class. It is equivalent to Parkland College's Chem 106 Organic Chemistry that is for the Healthcare students. I took the class myself two years ago. This class has 2,000 points of work in it. It has a tremendous amount of homework per unit (7 different areas - 5 of choice to do for each unit).

He recommended this as a stepping stone for a student who is unsure they are ready to tackle AP Chem. It would develop great study habits, due to its requirements. (I would think the student would learn their natural learning style pretty quickly too - the 7 different types of homework all lean towards a different learning style). AP Chem could then be taken during the senior year. This does separate the student from their fellow junior students. Puts them in the land of in between. They may need to make new relationships for study partners/help etc.

The instructor looked at this from an academic perspective. His goal is for them to learn. He teaches the class to pass the AP test. They students have to put in the time to accomplish that. The test is a bit like the ACT in the sense that they have to be able to apply the knowledge they learned to pass the test. It is not a light review of chemistry. He felt a 3 was a score that indicated they has learned a good foundation of chemistry.

I think Jim will keep the class. I have talked with him about the amount of work that will need to be done to gain a 4/5 on the AP test. It is in his hands now. I do not doubt he has the ability. It is a matter of him taking the time to do the work and study...

Thanks for your help.

Linda

Linda took the time to meet with the AP instructor that her son would have during the upcoming school year (this meeting took place in early August). The instructor clearly cared about the class and had been working on improving the course. I would encourage all parents to do what Linda did: be proactive and meet with teachers to learn about any challenging courses your student wants to take.

I shared responses from two different teachers. What a difference! The first teacher seemed apathetic in regard to improving the course while the second had already been making adjustments. I also want to point out that both teachers thought that their respective AP test was the hardest!

If your student is in an AP class and you learn that the school has below average percentages as previously described, then be proactive. Get AP prep books to use. Investigate online AP classes. Find out what other high schools are doing. Locate a great AP teacher at another school and pay them to tutor if they are available.

What should a student do if the family learns that the AP class is not effective as previously described? Should the student take the AP class or a regular class?

Talk to students who have been in the AP class and regular class. Better students take AP classes, so there tend to be less discipline issues. Teachers of AP classes tend to be more focused in those classes because they have the better students. The parents of AP students also tend to be more proactive and can put pressure on the administration to strengthen the AP class. If a student can get an A in the AP class then stay in the class. If a student most likely will get a C in the AP class and may get a low AP test score then I would seriously consider taking the regular class.

As mentioned earlier, if a student puts in the extra time preparing for the AP test then they can score well. This is a life lesson that applies to sports, school, the ACT, and AP tests.

Many colleges and universities offer college credit for AP test scores as well as placement into higher level college courses based on AP exam scores. The College Board website (CollegeBoard.org) lists which schools accept AP test scores and specifically how they use various AP tests and individual scores. The following is the University of Illinois' profile on the website as of November 27th, 2013.[16]

Exam Title	Min. Score Required	Number of Credits	Equivalent University Course
Biology	5	8	Integrative Biology 150 (4 hours) and Molecular & Cellular Biology 150 (4 hours)
Calculus AB	4	5	Math 220
Calculus BC	3	5	Math 220
	4	8	Math 220 and Math 231
Chemistry	3	3	Chemistry 102 (lecture only)
	4	6	Chemistry 102 and 104 (lecture only)
Chinese Language and Culture	4	10	Chinese 203 and 204
	5	20	Chinese 203, 204, 305, and 306

Comparative Government and Politics	5	3	Political Science 240
Computer Science A	3	3	CS 103
	4	3	CS 101
English Language and Composition	4	4	Rhetoric 105
English Literature and Composition	4	7	Rhetoric 105 and English 110
Environmental Science	4	3	Natural Resources and Environmental Sciences 100
European History	4	3	History 142
French Language and Culture	3	4	French 103
	4	8	French 103 and 104
	5	13	French 103, 104, 205, and 207
German Language and Culture	3	8	German 103 and 104
	4	11	German 103, 104 and 211
Human Geography	4	4	Geography 104
Italian Language and Culture	5	8	Italian103 and 104
Japanese Language and Culture	4	10	Japanese 203 and 204
	5	10	Japanese 203 and 204
Latin	3	8	Latin 103 and 104
	4	11	Latin 103, 104, and 199
Macroeconomics	4	3	Economics 103
Microeconomics	4	3	Economics 102
Music Theory	5	2	Music 101
Physics B	4	10	Physics 101 and 102

Physics C: Electricity and Magnetism	5	4	Physics 212
Physics C: Mechanics	5	4	Physics 211
Psychology	5	4	Psychology 100
Spanish Language	4	7	Spanish 141 and 200
	5	10	Spanish 141, 200, and 204
Spanish Literature and Culture	4	7	Spanish 141 and 200
	5	10	Spanish 141, 200, and 204
Statistics	4	3	Statistics 100
	5	6	Statistics 100 and 200
United States Government and Politics	4	3	Political Science 101
United States History	4	6	History 171 and 172
World History	4	3	History 100

This is just one example of a major university that rewards students for their strong AP test – not AP class – performance. Do not be afraid of AP tests. Just understand that they do require tremendous amounts of preparation because they are college level.

Dual-credit courses: For those not familiar with the term, it's a class offered at the high school that usually counts as a high school elective credit and a community college course. These are becoming more and more popular as technology improves and community colleges grow their outreach programs. Encourage your student to do as many of these as possible. I have had students finish one year of college before graduating from high school by taking advantage of these special courses. Not only do they give students a head start on college, but they lower the total cost of a college education because dual-credit courses are a small fraction of the cost of actually taking the course at a four-year university.

Le Roy High School is an excellent example of a public school system that gives their students an advantage because of dual-credit courses. Le Roy is located in Central Illinois, about 20 miles from Bloomington (national headquarters of State Farm Insurance) and 25 miles from Champaign (home of the University of Illinois). Le Roy is a small town with a population under 4,000 and the high school has an enrollment fewer than 250 students.

However, what they lack in numbers they make up for in leadership. Jeff Baughman, one of the administrators in the Le Roy School District, has been an advocate of dual-credit since day one. The following are his thoughts on how dual-credit has helped his students:

> *"Our percentage of students enrolled in dual credit varies year to year, but generally is around 25% of our juniors and seniors taking at least 6 credit hours per year. We have hit a high of 35% taking at least 6 hours. We currently offer 15 hours of dual credit on campus for free (Calculus - 5 hours, Finite Math - 4 hours, Composition 101 - 3 hours, and Composition 102 - 3 hours). Our advanced students can take at least 11 hours of dual credit for free on campus. We hope to offer 6 hours of social science within the next two years.*
>
> *Most of our students taking dual credit take courses online, such as PSYC 101, SOC 101, History, etc. It is common for our advanced students to take up to 25-30 hours before graduating between our courses and online courses. Online courses cost them tuition, fees, and books, but, if they plan to attend four year schools, they still come out*

ahead financially. On average, we estimate a Parkland course to cost about one-third of the cost of the same class at a four year university.

We have multiple students graduate every year and enter college as a sophomore. We have to keep a very close eye on what students take in relation to where they plan to go in order to make sure the courses they take transfer in their unique situation."

Dual credit courses are so popular at Le Roy that during the 2012-2013 school year they made a promotional video that can be seen at the following address: http://vimeo.com/58014954

If as student has to choose between a dual-credit course and an AP class, then I strongly encourage the student to choose the dual-credit course. An AP class is not a guarantee: college credit is only earned if an AP test score is high. A dual-credit course is a guarantee of earned college credit.

Top tier schools like Northwestern University, Washington University in St. Louis, and Ivy League schools will not accept dual-credit courses. However, schools with similar policies represent less than 5 percent of all colleges and universities. They may not give you college credit but they will enhance your college application.

Community College Courses: Community colleges are truly wonderful and can be an asset to a high school student. People can start taking community college courses when they are 16 years old. These could be evening, summer, or online classes.

I taught at a high school that was less than two miles from the local community college. Approximately, 10 percent of the senior class would graduate early in December. Many would then spend a semester at the community college, come back in May, attend graduation with their high school class, and then move on to their four year university. Every student I knew that did this said the same thing:

"Community college was harder than I expected."

Most assume a community college will just be like high school. It's not. It's like college because it is college. However, it helps students get a better understanding of what is to be expected when they truly go on to college. That's a good thing.

The goal of a college admissions office is to pick students they believe will succeed at the college level. The ACT, grades, and class rank certainly help but those represent high school performance.

High AP scores, dual-credit classes, and community college courses show a school that the student is already successfully doing college level work and is ready for college.

My daughter attends a small high school that doesn't offer much. Will she even be ready for college?

This is a great question. A high school does not make your student. A college will not make your student. The difference will be if your student truly maximizes the opportunities available regardless of the circumstances. I believe Julie's story confirms my point.

EMAIL: Attending a small school did not keep Julie from a guaranteed seat in medical school

It's Julie. I hope you remember me. I still have your "congratulations" note attached to my bulletin board from when I scored my 32 on my ACT! I have AWESOME news. I applied to three colleges in my process: U of I Champaign, U of I Chicago, and the University of Chicago. Just a few days after I had submitted my applications, I made the decision to not attend the University of Chicago because of the extremely high cost per year compared to the other two. I was accepted to both of the U of I's.

I then applied to the Honors College at the University of Illinois at Chicago (UIC). I interviewed and was almost immediately accepted. I decided then and there I really wanted to try the city life, so I accepted my offer and became a member of their Honor's College. Here is the AWESOME part.

I have wanted to become a doctor since I was two years old and part of the reason I applied to UIC was the amazing, hands-on research opportunities and resources for pre-med students. I also applied to their GPPA program. This program (Guaranteed Pre-Professional Admissions) offers a guaranteed seat in the U of I College of Medicine to a very select group of freshman students. You can only be accepted as a freshman and over 500 students applied this year. Only 20 were accepted. Based on my extracurricular activities, essay, oral essay, interview, and with emphasis on my ACT SCORE, I was one of those 20.

I will now begin my medical school classes next year and move to Champaign in 2018 to take my guaranteed seat in their Medical School and begin my training to become a pediatric oncologist.

All of this without the stress of the MCAT (I still take it, but my admissions are not based on it) and with TONS of medical opportunities beginning NEXT YEAR. I could NOT be more excited.

Lots of juniors feel the ACT will not matter that much in the end... my story proves it can be life changing years down the road as well as now! Thank you for helping me reach this goal! I have recommended you to everyone who asks!

Thanks again,
Julie

Julie's story is even more impressive when you consider where she came from. Her high school is a small rural school, her graduating class only had 67 students, offers no AP courses, only four dual-credit classes, and has no accelerated/honors program. She worked hard and maximized her ability at the school: ranked number one in her class and a four-year straight A student. Despite coming from a high school with limited opportunities, she was recognized as one of the best of the best.

College is the same way. The college does not make a person successful; it's the person that achieves success regardless of where they attend.

quiz day. He had a D in my class because he had not made up all his missed work prior to the end of the first quarter. I submitted the D for his first quarter grade. His family lawyer called the school and threatened to sue me and the school if he did not receive an A; he was ranked number one in his class at the time and worried about not being valedictorian. Fortunately, it was just a threat. The school supported me fully. David ended up with a C for the fall semester and still finished the school year as valedictorian.

I have also had parents call and ask what their student needed to do in order to perform better in my class. This is the type of call teachers want. Most teachers will work with you. However, let's assume the teacher offers no assistance. That's okay. At least the teacher knows you care. The best day of the school year for a teacher is the last day of school before summer vacation. One of the last things a teacher has to do is finalize grades. If a teacher knows you truly care about your grades and you are very close to the higher grade, the teacher may just give you the benefit of the doubt and change your grade to the higher mark. I've personally seen it happen many times.

Parents, encourage your student to talk to their high school teachers outside of school about academics. This is a good habit to develop in high school, because it is an essential habit to have in college. Professors and other college instructors will have office hours. It does take effort on the part of a college student to walk to the professor's office and coordinate a visit within one's daily schedule. However, it is worth it. 15 to 20 minutes with a high school teacher or college professor can really accelerate academic development.

Do not go in at the last minute to discuss the grade right before final exams. Teachers really dislike this. Track your grades, once you see

Chapter 13

Personal Statements & Essays

Most students do this part backwards. They begin working on their college applications first throughout the early fall semester and then start their personal statements and essays at the end, which is around October and November. That's too late.

> **This section is written to the student. Parents should also read it, but I want all readers to be clear who the audience is.**

End of Junior Year: Ask the best English teacher in your school if they would be willing to review your college application personal statement during the summer. Ask if you can email it to them. Teachers tend to have more free time in the summer to help. It will also put pressure on you to begin working on your statement during the summer.

Summer: Start with your personal statement. Many colleges want a personal statement. The University of Illinois, as an example, requests a personal statement as well as a writing prompt essay. Many schools do not post their writing prompts online until late summer (August 1ˢᵗ). There is time to work on the personal statement in the summer because school has not started yet. Trust me, when your senior year starts the time will fly by and before you know it November will have arrived.

I encourage all students to complete the Common Application. This is an application that is currently accepted at over 475 colleges and universities throughout the country. Every year more schools join the list. It's a very common sense approach to college applications: a student completes one application that is then sent to the desired schools on the list, so all the schools are looking at the same information. This will save your student a lot of time. The odds are that your student will be considering at least one college that accepts the Common Application.

The Common Application writing prompts really are personal statement prompts. This is the place to start.

The following are the instructions and essay prompts for the 2013 – 2014 Common Application (commonapp.org).

Instructions. The essay demonstrates your ability to write clearly and concisely on a selected topic and helps you distinguish yourself in your own voice. What do you want the readers of your application to know about you apart from courses, grades, and test scores? Choose the option that best helps you answer that question and write an essay of no more than 650 words, using the prompt to inspire and structure your response. Remember: 650 words is your limit, not your goal. Use the full range if you need it, but don't feel obligated to do so. (The application won't accept a response shorter than 250 words.)

• Some students have a background or story that is so central to their identity that they believe their application would be incomplete without it. If this sounds like you, then please share your story.

• Recount an incident or time when you experienced failure. How did it affect you, and what lessons did you learn?

• Reflect on a time when you challenged a belief or idea. What prompted you to act? Would you make the same decision again?

• Describe a place or environment where you are perfectly content. What do you do or experience there, and why is it meaningful to you?

• Discuss an accomplishment or event, formal or informal, that marked your transition from childhood to adulthood within your culture, community, or family.

First day of school: Ask the best English teacher in your school to review your updated drafts. Timing is so important. Teachers tend to have more time to work with students on something like this at the beginning of the school year. However, as the weeks go on, teachers have more responsibilities and grading to do AND other seniors begin asking them for help. Teachers only have so much time. School has to come first and helping seniors with personal statements and essays is technically not part of their duties.

Respect the teacher's time: Teachers are coming off summer vacation, so they tend to be in great moods when school starts. Teachers are not as busy at the start of a school year because there are no papers to grade, no major projects due, and classroom/school discipline issues are not mounting up. More importantly, most seniors are not even thinking about their essays or personal statements, so teachers are not being asked for help yet. However as the year goes on and seniors begin working on applications, they will start to ask teachers for help at the same time the teacher is starting to get very busy with school work. At some point, teachers will need to say "no" to students. You do not want to be stuck in this situation.

Review, review, review: You should have other trustworthy adults review the drafts. The more eyes that can review the drafts and provide feedback the better they will be in the end. Parents should definitely read them. Your parents know you, know your strengths, and can help you play up your strengths as some students may want to be modest. This is not the time for modesty.

Beware. It's too easy to ask your friends. You may have a friend that is a great writer who can offer constructive advice and that's great. However, the people at the universities reading the essays and personal statements are adults, much older than a high school student. The material needs to be tested on people of similar age.

PARENT WARNING: Colleges can easily spot when someone else has written the essay. As a parent, you are just there for guidance, not to write it for them.

This is NOT one and done: Nationally, writing skills have dramatically decreased among public school students. Texting has taught students how NOT to write. Unfortunately, many students think that good writing is putting together one rough draft, have a teacher review it, correct it, and then submit the final version. In too many schools what I just described would "earn" at least a B grade. You don't want to submit a "B" personal statement or essay.

This is going to be the most important writing you are going to do during your high school years. There should be at least four drafts – ideally six – making sure every little mistake is caught while verifying the essay is clear and concise. This takes time, multiple drafts, various people reading and providing suggestions, and you need to be humble enough to listen and learn how to improve your work. This is REAL writing.

RECOMMENDATION: The more professional eyes that read the essays the better which is why I recommend asking an English teacher. I also recommend Katie Keown, a professional editor living in the Chicago area. She is phenomenal and has worked with many of my ACT students.

Katie can correctly guide a student from start to finish or simply review an essay that has already been edited and is near finalization. Not only will your student have a more professional personal statement and essays in the end, but your student will learn how to be a better writer which is invaluable. If you would like additional information about Katie's services, her email is **KatieKeown11@gmail.com**.

There are no "do over's": Once the personal statements and essays are submitted then that is it. Depending on the situation, many people may be reading them. An essay submitted in, say, October may be read in November, December, January, or even February, especially if you are being considered for honors programs and special scholarships offered by the school.

Essays can be game changers: Tell a story. Personal statements and essays show the real you: how you think, how you view the world, your maturity level, your growth, your goals, and your objectives. You can learn a lot by reading someone's personal writings. Colleges want to learn about you!

I was a high school math teacher when I taught in the public schools; however, my mission was to prepare students to be better test performers which I knew would better prepare them for college. Therefore, toward the end of my teaching career as I continued to improve, I had my students read business books and write papers related to business ideas and plans. (I designed an Algebra 2 curriculum that focused completely on the business world that way my students would never be able to ask, "When will we ever use this?" Hence, the reading and writing material being business specific.) The first time I experimented with the writing concept was late in the fall semester.   The first writing assignment was to write about starting a small business that they could realistically see themselves wanting to do in the future. One paper impressed me.   The student's name was Cassie.

Cassie was an average student, had a C in my class, never talked in class, and was extremely polite. Because of those qualities, I didn't really know her outside of her math performance on various tests and quizzes. However, when I read her first paper I was astonished by how much this quiet girl had to say. She was so detailed and her writing style was phenomenal. She wanted to be an interior designer and discussed how she grew up rearranging the furniture in her parent's home and was always drawing room designs. After reading her assignment, I had an immediate connection with her because I too grew

162

up rearranging my parent's furniture and still enjoy drawing house plans to this day.

When I shared this connection with Cassie, she immediately smiled and began to ask me questions. We joked about how we drove our parents crazy with new furniture arrangements. Cassie began participating more in my class on a regular basis. I was no longer a teacher; I was an adult who respected her dreams. Cassie was no longer a quiet C student, but someone who had similar interests with me. A college should gain a similar sense of connection from your personal statements and essays.

The smaller the school the more important the writing becomes. The University of Illinois had over 35,000 students apply for admissions during the fall of 2013[17]. UCLA had almost 100,000 students[18]. I'm sure the essays are read but not necessarily easily remembered. Smaller schools, especially private universities, take the writings very seriously, in part because they have a lot less students applying. An admissions officer may read your personal statement two or three times and then ask questions about it during a meeting. Again, you need to take this part of the college application process very seriously.

Don't take the last paragraph lightly. A high school guidance counselor shared a story with me that a straight A student with a 36 composite ACT score was denied admission to a Big Ten university because the student wrote a one sentence response to what was supposed to be a 300 word essay prompt response. Every part of the application process is important.

Help for Emily

Emily took my ACT classes twice: in the fall of her junior year and the summer before her senior year. She also had to drive over 90 minutes one-way to get to the class. That's dedication. Emily's family also attended the parent seminar the summer before her senior year.

Emily did everything I suggested. She got her essay done early and she asked a teacher for help the first week of school. Six weeks later I was contacted by Emily. The teacher had still not gotten back with ways on how to improve her draft and the essay was due in a week for a scholarship she was applying for at Southern Illinois University in Edwardsville. She was in a jam and needed help. I agreed to help her for a few reasons.

1. I admire anyone who is willing to drive that far to attend my ACT classes.

2. She was a model student in class and constantly participated.

3. She implemented everything I taught in my classes including reading non-fiction material on a daily basis. She reaped the results as her ACT score from her first test to her last test jumped a total of 7 composite points and 11 points on the reading test. I was very proud of her.

4. She agreed to let me share the drafts with my classes and seminar participants in order to help others understand the editing process.

She truly is a wonderful young lady and I cannot say enough about how impressive she is as a person.

> **NOTE**: I included the previous paragraph because I do not want to receive requests for help in this area. I have six children, teach ACT classes' year around, have an online ACT class, and conduct parent seminars. In short, my schedule is already full. Thank you for understanding and respecting my time. Again, I recommend contacting Katie Keown.

The next page begins with the first rough draft Emily sent me.

Experiences That Influence My Life

My name is ████████████. Attending ██████████ High School has provided me with numerous opportunities that influence my life daily. Since the age of seven, becoming a dentist has been my dream; SIUE can make this dream a reality. SIUE will provide me with everything necessary for my education from the beautiful campus to the amazing programs available. In high school, my determined work ethic has enabled me to excel. All of my dedication and effort will help me reach my fullest potential to make my dreams come true. As the eldest of three children, being a positive influence and role model for my siblings has played a major role in my life. My experience and leadership has helped me become an independent person who is not easily influenced by the crowd. As a student, I have distinguished myself, from others by my independence, leadership, and experiences, and it is these qualities which will allow me to reach my fullest potential at SIUE.

The Church blessed me with an opportunity to attend a Catholic event called World Youth Day. Along with other parishioners, I visited Madrid, Spain and Rome, Italy. In addition, I was able to reunite with relatives in Germany for two weeks, before my classmates arrived. My trip began by maneuvering around an international airport unaccompanied at the age of fifteen. In Germany, it was important to learn about my heritage and how Germans live. I learned that the German culture is very different from the United States. For example, students have more independence and adults have less control over children. This made me realize how fortunate we are and to appreciate the respect we have for one another. This circumstance made me become completely aware of my responsibilities and decisions. Once arriving in Rome with my classmates, what became important to me was the responsibility of knowing where my belongings were at all times and helping those around me. On this trip, my friends began to refer to me as a caretaker for always looking out for their best interest. As a student on this trip, the importance of time management, independence and the diversity of cultures became a major part of my life.

As a student at SIUE my goals are to become involved with others and make a positive impact on those around me. In high school, participating in basketball, cheerleading, track, and cross country has had a tremendous impact on my life. Being the captain of the cross country team has allowed my leaderships qualities to flourish, from encouraging my teammates with pep talks to organizing practices. My team has become my second family; they are the people who influence my life and help motivate me day to day. It is important to step up as a senior and take responsibility to maintain the positive reputation my school has worked hard to achieve.

I am an outstanding listener and supportive of others. These personal quality traits are what distinguished me from the other fifty-two students in my class to be selected as a leader for a highly respected religious retreat. On this retreat my responsibilities included influencing classmates in a positive manner and helping them to see themselves as pillars of the community. It was important to find these qualities within myself and help others see them in themselves. While some people saw this as too much pressure, I felt this was an enlightening experience that will help me grow in faith and confidence. The responsibilities of this experience have helped me become better at prioritizing and time management. The honor of being chosen for this experience has helped me grow as a leader by learning to respect others, to respect myself and to see how others perceive me.

The college application process has brought me to the realization that we as Americans can be anything we want to be, with hard work, dedication, individuality and responsibility. With these characteristics I, ▮▮▮▮▮▮▮▮▮▮, believe I am the perfect candidate for this scholarship. My contributions to SIUE and its student body will help make an ideal community, while filling the world with educated, young optimistic adults.

First Rough Draft

Don't be school specific. In the first, third, and last paragraphs Emily mentions a specific university. That's not necessary. They know all about themselves; they want to learn about your student. Most personal statements and essays have word limits, so don't waste any on a particular school. The essay should also be written in a way that easily allows it to be used for multiple schools and scholarships. We don't want the student to "reinvent the wheel" once a great personal statement or essay has been created.

Focus. Emily has a specific event that had an impact on her life. She needed to go into greater detail about the entire experience and connect it back to her growth as a person which has brought her to her current state today. It could be an event, a personal challenge like a disability, or overcoming an obstacle.

Review, review, and review. Within a one week period Emily and I went through six drafts with the final review a few hours before the essay had to be mailed off. It was a very stressful week because Emily and I live almost two hours from each other, so all contact was via email or phone while working around her school schedule and my evening ACT classes.

This is why it is so important to start writing personal statements and essays before the school year begins. They take time. This is why you want to seek out help from an English teacher during the first week of school. Make sure you make specific arrangements to follow-up with the teacher. I have had quite a few students who were promised help by a teacher. The teacher did not follow up, got busy, and the promised help never materialized.

Final Draft

On the following page is Emily's final draft. If you take the time to read both drafts, I believe you will see the difference. The first draft is an essay that most college essay help books would suggest writing. In short, it is the average high school student essay. We don't want your student to produce an average essay. The goal is to create an outstanding essay.

Emily's final draft gives any reader a clear understanding of how this particular event impacted Emily. If you read this today and met Emily tomorrow, you both could easily have a sincere conversation about this particular trip. That is what your student wants. Give the college or university something that is so specific that they can discuss it with you in great detail. It makes your student more memorable and that is the goal.

The Experience That Influenced My Life

The sum of one's life experiences helps to define a person. World Youth Day in Madrid, Spain during the summer of 20█ provided numerous experiences that increased my faith and helped me grow as a person. The event began with a challenge before I ever crossed the ocean: writing a letter to the priest asking for acceptance to this special event. Waiting for a response took patience and receiving my acceptance letter was such a relief.

My duties began with fundraising. This process took two years and included several different tasks from making pies to setting up formal dinners. As a student my responsibility was to be prompt and prepared for any challenge encountered. Parents - mine and others - noticed my leadership efforts and began relying on me more. At meetings, it was important to work well with others and remain focused. At the time, fundraising was frustrating. My friends had parents sell items for them at work. Meanwhile, I went door to door selling products and taking the initiative to be persuasive to uphold my duty. This taught me to extend my comfort zone and take part in experiences that helped me develop as a person.

This trip would also provide an opportunity to reunite with relatives in Germany. As a fifteen-year-old, it was a challenge maneuvering around an international airport alone. In Germany, taking the train and surviving in the world independently became a daily task. This made me realize the importance of communication to prevent confusion.

While attending a German high school with my cousin, my respect for others grew. I was astonished at the students' disrespectful behavior: skipping classes and contradicting or making fun of teachers. I will never forget telling students how different my school was and punishments we would receive if we behaved in a disrespectful manner. Students began judging me with numerous American stereotypes: my actions were a reflection of all American teenagers. This taught me to be a positive influence and leader in order to make an impact on others. I became an independent thinker and thought outside the box, learning not to second guess my instincts.

Students in Germany do anything for people to like them or to be part of the crowd. This never appealed to me. Watching others, I observed their mistakes and learned. The only thing important to me was growing into a better person. My interests and morals developed because of these experiences. I realized it was more important to stick out for the right reasons rather than being satisfied with being a typical everyday student.

After leaving Germany and traveling independently to Madrid, it was a relief to see classmates. Traveling as part of a large group emphasized the importance of responsibility, not only for myself and my own belongings but for the safety and welfare of my friends as well. A turning point arose when a classmate was robbed. Reminding her that she lost only material possessions was a successful but difficult task.

My beliefs continued to develop and became even more important to me. In Europe, we visited numerous churches and basilicas. Everyday a new learning experience taught me how to become a better person by helping others. Despite being the youngest student on the trip, I seemed to be one of the most responsible. Classmates began to refer to me as a caretaker because I was constantly looking out for their best interests: calling to make sure they had not overslept or reminding them to bring certain belongings for the day. My experience in traveling led others to watch my actions and ask me for advice in times of need.

As a leader, it is important to be a positive influence and role model. As a student on this trip, the importance of hard work, dedication, independence, and responsibility enabled me to stand out from other students. Experiences such as the one described have contributed to my development as a person. I would appreciate consideration for this scholarship which will provide me with even more opportunities for continued personal development.

Chapter 14

Letters of Recommendation

Your essays and personal statements are you writing stories about you. Letters of recommendation (LOR) are others writing stories about you. This part can be challenging because you cannot directly control the content. However, the following is a basic framework that will make this portion much easier.

Get Ten. Your student should ask ten individuals who know them well to write a letter of recommendation. These people could be teachers, employers, neighbors, church officials, coaches or adults your student respects. Ask a variety of different people. A teacher will provide an academic perspective about the student. An employer will most likely provide insight on the student's work ethic that is different from what a teacher might include. A church official may focus on moral character and how your student matured over the years.

Why so many? Although your student will choose people they truly respect, most likely the student does not know how well they write. If you receive an LOR that is not written well, you do not want to feel obligated to use it and you do not want to offend the person who took the time to write it. Most college and universities will ask for only one or two at the most three, so having ten gives your student flexibility to pick the best ones to submit.

It may be hard to think of ten different people to write a letter or recommendation. Parents can help provide suggestions on who to ask. The following may help spur some thoughts.

- Three high school teachers
- High school coaches
- High school band, choir, play and orchestra directors
- High school guidance counselor
- High school principal
- Current employer
- Former employer
- Family who hired you to babysit their children
- Club sponsor
- Church official
- Club coach
- Private tutor: academic, athletic, or music
- Mentor

Give writers time. When I taught in the public schools many students would ask me to write letters of recommendation. It took me two weeks to write one. I wanted to make sure it was correct and truly conveyed a picture of the student. Your student wants great letters of recommendation, so be respectful of the time it takes to write a quality story about your student. At the same time, make it clear that you will check in two weeks later. Two weeks is plenty of time. Most adults will appreciate and respect your timeline. It's also okay to have your student check in a week later just to politely remind them about the letter of recommendation.

Your student needs to be proactive requesting and gathering the letters of recommendations. Parents should not be doing this for their student. This is part of the growing up process and preparing young people for the independence necessary to be successful in college.

Review. I always gave a draft to the student before finalizing it. One, I wanted to make sure they knew what I wrote about them, because some schools may ask the student questions about the content of a letter or recommendation. Two, I wanted to make sure I had correctly included every detail. If you receive an LOR that contains a factual error, don't be afraid to politely point it out to the writer. Remember the writer respects you, which is why they are taking the time to write the LOR in the first place. They want it to be factually accurate as much as you do. If there are factual errors then you honestly cannot submit it to a college, which would make it useless. This means you would have wasted the writer's time because you were afraid to point out the error. That's not fair to the writer or you.

 Ten signed copies. Once the student approved the draft and I was satisfied, I gave them ten signed copies even though I never had a student ask for that many. I learned over time to do this. I cannot tell you how many times I would have a student come into my room five minutes before class requesting a signed copy of the letter of recommendation for a school or scholarship they just heard about and they needed to send off the application that very same day. By giving the student plenty of extra copies that made both of our lives a lot easier. Again, the writer respects you, which is why they are taking the time to write an LOR for you. Politely ask for ten signed copies. If you know you will be applying to a lot of schools then ask for more.

NOTE: Every student is different. Some students will apply to only three schools while I have known others that applied to more than ten schools. For most students ten LOR copies should be enough. However, if you are going to apply to five schools ask for 15 signed LOR copies. If you are going to apply to seven schools then ask for 20 signed LOR copies.

- Minimum: 10 copies
- Between: number of schools you expect to apply to x 3
- Maximum: 20 copies

Keep copies for the future. When I taught in the public schools I had a student named Lexi who had me write a letter of recommendation and was accepted to a phenomenal university. During the spring semester of her junior year of college I received a phone call from Lexi's mom. The junior year of college - like the junior year of high school – is very challenging and students are dealing with the added emotions of realizing they are almost done with this phase of life which they recently just got comfortable with.

Her mom gave me an update on Lexi, but the original intent of the call was to ask if I could email them a copy of the letter of recommendation I wrote. Lexi's mom knew her daughter needed an encouragement at that particular time in her life. Apparently it helped, because a received an uplifting phone message from Lexi the following week. As humans sometimes we need a reminder of our strengths and accomplishments and letters of recommendations can do that.

A well-written letter of recommendation can do wonders for a student and their family. They can serve as motivation, encouragement, as well as exhortations depending on the circumstances. I watched many students tear up as they read letters of recommendation. I have had parents visit me at school to thank me in person for a letter of recommendation because it meant so much to them as parents.

Example. I have included a copy of Lexi's letter of recommendation I wrote NOT because I believe I am a great writer, but because when I was first asked to write letters of recommendations I knew I was not. I received many requests to write letters of recommendations, in part because I have a "story teller" presentation style whether I am teaching an ACT class or conducting a seminar. I use stories to solidify points. However, I was not confident in my ability to write letters of recommendations, so I sought help from a great mentor teacher, Mr. Stan Yanchus.

Stan graciously took the time to teach me how to write letters of recommendation. He taught me to be very specific and detailed. He showed me how to incorporate personal stories and anecdotes about the student. He instructed me on how to keep the focus on the student. In short, he taught me how to make a letter of recommendation stick out from the average letter of recommendation written by most high school teachers.

Stan knew all of this because he was a great English teacher who was constantly developing his abilities. He was a great story teller, a captivating teacher, and received A LOT of letter of recommendation requests from students. He learned how to write quality recommendations from the very people who read them: college admissions officers.

Writing a personal statement is very similar to how you want someone to write a letter of recommendation for you. A personal statement is you telling a story about yourself. A letter of recommendation is someone telling a story about you.

I am sharing the upcoming LOR example because this is what your student should be looking for from the writer. As an example, most students will ask high school teachers. Say Jessica asks her favorite high school teacher Ms. Smith for a letter of recommendation. Not a problem, Ms. Smith says come in tomorrow and it will be ready. Jessica is excited.

After Jessica leaves, Ms. Smith goes to her computer, pulls up her letter of recommendation form letter, changes the name to Jessica, updates the grade to reflect Jessica's grade, verifies that the pronouns match Jessica's gender, adds a few personal notes about Jessica, and then the letter is finished. The next day Jessica gets the letter of recommendation and it looks just like all the others. Ironically, Jessica like most students is happy that the teacher got it done so quickly.

Unfortunately, the above happens very often. Teachers are busy and many have learned how to speed up various processes including letters of recommendations. I have personally seen the above happen to hundreds of students. This is another reason your student should get ten different letters of recommendations. Encourage your student to select people who will tell a story about the student. It will be worth it.

NOTE: I want to make a point that I am not attempting to criticize teachers who do what I just described. I understand why they do it. Say a high school has 400 seniors. Those 400 seniors are most likely all going to be asking the same teachers for letters of recommendations. During my last few years of teaching in the public schools, I would get well over 30 requests. I spent at least two hours on each one from start to finish. That's 60 hours. I also turned down a lot of students because I did not have time or did not have a specific story to share about that particular student. In short, I had to say "no."

There are teachers who have a hard time saying "no" to students. Teachers enter the profession because they want to help young people. It's our nature. Therefore, some teachers figure out a way to speed up the process in order to keep everyone happy. Unfortunately, that's not good enough for your student. A college admissions official can recognize a "form" letter of recommendation just like they can tell when a student didn't write their own personal statement.

If you are not sure what teachers to ask, check with people who recently graduated from your high school. Ask if you could read the letters of recommendations written by teachers you are considering. This will give you a better idea of who to ask.

Fall of 20█

To Whom It May Concern:

I had the pleasure of having ████████████████ High School senior ████████████████ in my Algebra 2 class last year. During my ten years of teaching, I have never had a student demonstrate so much perseverance and determination in overcoming both test and math anxiety as Lexi did in Algebra 2.

Lexi struggled through the basic Algebra review unit from the first day of math class last year. After four weeks of poor performance I recommended to her that she transfer to a lower level math course. She was determined not to transfer, however. I told her that in order to succeed in Algebra she would need to come in before school for help on a daily basis until she caught up with the rest of the class.

This was a problem for Lexi because she was a swimmer who practiced before school. Lexi, therefore, faced a major choice: transfer to a lower level math class or quit swimming in order to come in for help. In spite of her love for the sport, Lexi quit swimming and began coming to school thirty minutes early in order to face the challenge of mastering Algebra.

Lexi pulled her grade from a 35% up to a 72% by the end of the semester. Although she struggled throughout the fall semester, she continued to progress as she learned to enjoy math. Furthermore, she overcame her fear of taking tests, learned to prepare for them, and developed strategies to be more efficient at taking tests. She also displayed her maturity by reviewing tests and learning from her mistakes rather than allowing temporary failures to stop her from achieving her goals.

At the end of the fall semester, in spite of her success, I recommended to Lexi once again that she transfer to a lower level math class for the spring semester. The second semester of Algebra 2 is much harder than the fall semester, and I was not sure Lexi could yet keep up with the pace. I was wrong! Not only did Lexi keep up, but she surpassed her fall semester performance and earned an 83% for the spring semester. Even more amazing than her eventual success was the fact that her perseverance and commitment testify to both her character and potential for success. She came in for help before school (thirty minutes early) over 100 days during the school year.

This year Lexi is the captain of the school's swim team. When the team is not practicing in the morning, Lexi still comes in for help from her trigonometry teacher. This young lady, who I thought could not handle Algebra 2, came to my room the other day and told me she earned an 89% (B+) on her first trigonometry test. Lexi's successes have taught me to never question the power of human potential to learn, especially when a student is willing to commit and dedicate herself like Lexi did. Obviously, ▮▮▮▮▮▮ is the type of student who will enhance the educational atmosphere wherever she is.

The restrictions of time and space inherent in a recommendation letter prevent me from even scratching the surface about the potential of this remarkable young lady. Please contact me if you wish additional information.

Sincerely,

Jason Franklin

Jason Franklin, National Board Certified Math Teacher

▮▮▮▮▮ High School

Home: ▮▮▮▮▮▮   School: 217.351.3951

▮▮▮▮@champaignschools.org

This was definitely NOT a form letter of recommendation. Form letters of recommendations are obvious to spot as they have big margins, a lot of spacing, and still only take up about half a page. I was struggling to get everything to fit on one page.

Lexi was not an A student. Too often students think they can only ask teachers of class in which they earned an A. The college is not going to care about the grade – they already have a copy of your high school transcript. Lexi was failing my class, had to choose between transferring to a lower math class or quit swimming, and chose to put grades before athletics.

Was she rewarded for her decision? Not only did she get a C in the fall semester followed by a B in the spring, the following year the swim team made her captain because of the mature decision she made the year before. That says a lot about how she handled the entire situation as she earned the respect of her teammates in a way no one could have predicted. More importantly, she learned the value of asking for help outside of school, which was made evident with her trigonometry class the following year.

Chapter 15

Resume Portfolio

Most college applications have a section where a student is asked to list extra-curricular activities and accomplishments. The space usually includes a few lines. If your student can make their first three years of high school fit on those few small lines, then your student is in trouble! Your student needs to create a resume portfolio and include it with college application.

How can a student meet the criteria for getting in? She works and lacks in community service.

Most schools limit the criteria to very objective measures already discussed in this book. Work is a fantastic resume enhancer because a job provides experiences that other extra-curricular activities do not. The key is taking what the student does – in this case the work experience – and share how this has helped prepare the student for college.

I had a home school student who had a dog walking business. Her work started every morning at 5:30 A.M. She was in my Christmas Break classes that started at 9 A.M. One day it was snowing pretty badly, but we still had class. She showed up a little late and explained that it took her a little longer to walk the dogs. She had organized her business on her own. That's impressive.

I had another student who operated his own lawn mowing business. He had so many clients that he hired a few of his friends to help him and even needed to purchase bigger machinery because of all his clients. He made over $10,000 just during the summer months. Then, when he went away to college, he sold his lawn mowing business.

The above examples can easily be highlighted in a resume portfolio. The following are steps to get started.

Step #1: Get a copy of the student's high school transcript immediately after the junior year is over. It should include the grade point average (weighted and non-weighted), class rank (weighted and non-weighted), and size of the student's graduating class. If the transcript does not include any of this, then ask the student's guidance counselor or registrar for the information. All grades, class ranks, etc. are computerized now, so it should take no time to get.

Step #2: On a computer list all the activities the student has participated in during the first three years of high school: school sports, club sports, church activities, jobs held, and any other groups. They do not necessarily have to be school sponsored activities.

Step #3: Under each activity list specifics associated with each item. For example, if the student was a cheerleader, did they coach any cheerleading camps for younger girls, did they attend any competitions, how did the team perform at those competitions, did they conduct any fundraising for the team, etc.

List what the team/group accomplished as well as what the student accomplished. For example, being a starter on a football team is nice, but if the student was a starter on a team that won a state championship that is quite different.

Step #4: Do any of the accomplishments require a brief summary in order to bring more clarity? Assume that the adult looking at your resume portfolio has no idea what the purpose of the organization is. For example, some schools have student councils that only organize homecoming activities while other schools have student councils that meet with school administrators, attend school board meetings, and are actively involved in representing the concerns of the student body.

Step #5: Gather pictures associated with various activities and schedule your senior pictures during the summer, so they can be used as well. Having worked with thousands of students, I have seen a lot of fantastic and creative senior pictures. Every year I marvel at the quality of these photographs. You want to be able to use them on your portfolio, which means they need to be scheduled in the summer. You can always switch pictures on the resume portfolio as better ones become available.

Step #6: Based on the above, determine if your resume portfolio will be two pages or four pages. If you don't have a lot of information, then use two. Don't feel the need to do four pages. The key is quality, not quantity. Start with your contact information and a good face picture at the top on the front page. Then follow with your academic record because most colleges are going to want to know that first. The rest of the layout will depend on what you have accomplished as well as the variety.

Step #7: After you have put the resume portfolio together and have the final version then have them printed on cardstock paper in color. If you are doing a two page portfolio, then have it printed on both sides, so you are giving the school one sheet. If you are doing a four page portfolio, then have it printed on 11 x 17" cardstock paper and then fold it into a booklet.

Once you have the resume portfolio completed, send it the admissions office, so it becomes a part of your student file. When visiting schools, take a copy with you and give it to an admissions officer. If you are going to attend a college fair, take several copies, so you can pass them out to colleges. If there is a college visiting your high school, take a copy to the meeting and when the meeting ends introduce yourself to the college representative and hand them your resume portfolio.

The resume portfolio is part of your first impression to people who may never meet you like those who serve on a scholarship committee and will only see what is in your student file. Make it count!

EXAMPLE: There is a seminar DVD that supplements this book. On the DVD you will see an excellent example of a resume portfolio that was put together by Rachel Smith. Rachel has helped many students with resume portfolios. If you would additional information about her services or would like an example sent to you, email Rachel at **Rachel.Smith.04@hotmail.com**. If you would like to purchase a seminar DVD, go to BetterPrepSuccess.com or contact me at Jason.Franklin@BetterPrepSuccess.com.

Chapter 16

Individual Visits

Let me tell you a story about Lisa and Sara. I had both girls in my ACT class at the same time. Both girls wanted to go to the University of Illinois and study accounting. Both girls had the same ethnic background.

Lisa was an above average hard working student. She got A's and B's, but was not ranked in the top 20 percent, and had ACT scores of 20 then 22 and then 24. She worked very hard to get the 24. On the other hand, Sara was ranked in the top 10 of her class, was a straight A student, and scored two 27's on her first two tests and then a 30 after taking my ACT class.

At the time, the U of I accounting program wanted students with at least a 29 ACT and ranked in the top 10 percent of their class. Sara was safe while Lisa was not. Lisa understood. She was just hoping to get wait listed and then possibly earn a spot later. Both applied during the fall of their senior years.

One night, I was teaching an ACT class and Lisa showed up at the classroom door. She was crying and signaling for me to come talk to her. Once I got the class started on a drill, I went to see what was wrong. Before I could say anything, she gave me a big hug and said, "I got in!" I started crying (which was very hard to explain to my class when I returned to the room). I was so proud of her.

A week later I was visiting Sara's high school and saw her in the hallway, so I asked for an update. She was depressed because she was waitlisted by the U of I. I was shocked! Lisa got in but Sara did not. Lisa the A/B students with an ACT composite of 24 got in, but Sara the straight A student with a 30 did not. It did not make sense. Sara was clearly the stronger student. I began asking Sara questions and at one point she gave me the wrong answer.

Jason: "Sara, did you ever visit the U of I?"

Sara: "No. I didn't need to."

Jason: "You never visited?"

Sara: "I didn't need to. They have always been my number one choice."

Jason: "You never visited?"

Sara: "I don't understand why you keep asking me that?"

Jason: "Sara, how far do you live from the campus?"

Sara: "About five blocks."

And there was the problem. As mentioned before, the U of I recently has had over 30,000 students apply every year. Students are truly a number. The admissions office has to go through applications quickly. Imagine for a moment that that admissions officers are meeting and reviewing applications. At some point they got to Sara's application and someone asks the others if anyone knows Sara. Since Sara never visited, no one knew her. They then checked her application. It asks if she had ever visited the campus. Sara marked "no." Then I am sure they noticed her address and that she only lived a few blocks from campus. What message did Sara send the U of I?

"I don't really want to come to your school.
If I did care, I would have walked a few blocks and visited."

Sara did want to go to the U of I but the school had no way of knowing based on just her college application. Unfortunately, Sara sent the wrong message.

Back to Lisa. At some point in a similar meeting the group got to Lisa's application. Again, someone asked if anyone knew Lisa. Someone in the room raised their hand and said yes, because Lisa visited the campus **five times** and made arrangements for each visit with the same admissions officer. This then allowed the officer to explain the purpose of each visit.

Visit #1: Lisa and her parents met with the admissions officer (the one who is now sharing information about the visits). This admissions officer is now Lisa's advocate, whom Lisa created because of her visits, explains that Lisa has always wanted to go to the U of I; it's her dream school. Lisa's mom and dad both attended the U of I; in fact, that is where they originally met and the family has always lived in Champaign. Lisa grew up attending U of I athletic events. She wants to study accounting like her dad, whose firm in town provides internships to U of I seniors. The advocate arranged the other visits and went on to summarize each. The visits were on different days going back to the spring of her junior year.

Visit #2: Lisa and her dad met with the Director of Financial Aid. Lisa's parents were covering a part of Lisa's college expenses, but Lisa would have to pay for the rest, so the family wanted to know what resource might be available: grants, work-study programs, loans, etc.

Visit #3: Lisa and her dad met with the head of the accounting program. Her dad wanted to learn how the accounting program had changed since he attended the U of I and what internship opportunities would be available to Lisa in the future.

Visit #4: Lisa wanted to watch a specific accounting professor teach a class, so arrangements were made to come over one afternoon when her high school had a half day of school and sit in on one of the professor's classes. They then met for about 15 minutes after the class to talk about the U of I accounting program.

Visit #5: Lisa wanted to know what it was like to be a U of I student for a day. Arrangements were made for Lisa to meet a senior majoring in accounting for breakfast. The senior then took Lisa with her to all of her classes for that day and discussed the U of I and the accounting program.

Who really wanted to attend the U of I: Sara or Lisa?

Colleges want to give acceptance letters to students that they believe will accept the invitation. Top tier schools like the U of I do not want to be bargaining chips. They don't want to be the back-up school. This is why you hear stories of top students getting denied admissions or waitlisted to top schools. In many cases, the school figured out that they were not the number one choice.

If you are looking at five schools then each school must feel like they are your number one choice, because in reality they may be. You don't know what is going to happen. Your personal rankings will change numerous times throughout your journey.

I share Lisa's story understanding that it is an extreme example; you should not need to visit a campus five times unless it is close. Lisa's family only lived 15 minutes from the U of I campus, so it was easy to set up the visits. However, if you are looking at a college that is several hours away then you need to maximize your time each day you are on the campus. Rely on phone calls and emails in order to make it clear to the school that you are really want to come to their school.

Getting Started

This section is written directly to the students. You need to meet with a college admissions officer **BEFORE** applying to interested schools. When applying to colleges, you are just a number. An individual meeting changes you from a number to a real person. Many top colleges eliminate students because they have not visited the campus **PRIOR** to applying.

If you are serious about an out-of-state school, then you must visit. Many out-of-state public universities limit how many out-of-state students they will accept, so those spots become much more competitive. Colleges also know that many students apply to out-of-state schools with no real intention of considering the school. The student just wants to see if they will get accepted. By visiting an out-of-state school, the student sends a strong message:

"I WAS WILLING TO GIVE UP TIME AND MONEY TO VISIT YOUR SCHOOL BECAUSE I REALLY WANT TO BE ADMITTED."

A visit allows you to share stories, explain your academic record, and describe yourself in a way that a college application and essays cannot. The college admission officer gets to know the real you while putting a face to a name.

Prepare for the Meeting

Dress well. This should be obvious, but you would be surprised. My ACT classes held at Illinois Wesleyan University used to be in a building adjacent to the admissions office. Our room had big windows that made up at least 60 percent of the wall. In the summer I watched visiting high school students and parents walk by as they took a tour of the campus with a college student.

One summer I stopped my class and had all the students look out the window. Walking by on a tour was a high school girl dressed so inappropriately you would have thought she was a prostitute. Then her mom went by and she was dressed as poorly as her daughter. The whole class was laughing which most likely meant the admissions office was also laughing. I told the class that I could almost guarantee that the girl will be denied acceptance to IWU. If she is going to dress so inappropriately on a visit, what would happen if she actually attended the school?

Appearance matters. Avoid dressing like a typical high school student. Don't wear tight clothes (especially girls); it's distracting. Avoid too much make-up. Dress conservatively. Most of the people you meet will be adults and as people age they tend to become more naturally conservative. Keep in mind that you will most likely do a lot of walking, so wear an outfit that is nice but comfortable enough to move around (girls, don't wear heals. You will regret it!).

No cell phone. Leave your cell phone in the car. Don't carry it with you. I work with over 1,000 high school students each year, and I can tell you that most teenagers are addicted to their cell phones and check them without even realizing it. I have had admissions officers tell me that they have been in meeting with families where a student was texting or checking the cell phone (they've also seen parents do the same thing). That's rude! Be cautious and leave the cell phone behind. You will survive a few hours without it.

Bring parents. This sends a message: my parents support me and are interested in me attending your school. Most colleges assume your parents will be helping you financially, and they would like to meet the investors.

I had a student once named John. He scored a 34 on his ACT and wanted to attend the University of Illinois and become a veterinarian. I met with John and his mom to go over his test analysis. His mom was a talker. At one point, I looked at John and said,

"John, you will have no problem getting into the U of I academically.
Your problem is you have no personality."

If you got the seminar DVD that complements this book and have already watched it, then you saw how I perform in front of a classroom. I tell stories to solidify concepts. I use humor when appropriate. John sat in my class for fourteen weeks and did not crack a smile. Even when I told him in front of his mom that he had no personality, John with a straight face said, "You're right."

My concern was that John's mom would dominate the meeting and John would just sit there. Parents can ask questions and participate in the meeting, but the student needs to lead the meeting and demonstrate independence from mom and dad.

I told John the truth about his personality because I cared. A week earlier I had met with one of the heads of the pre-vet program at the U of I because his son happened to be in my ACT class. I asked him what the U of I looked for in a pre-vet student. He told me that they had actually been reviewing their admissions policy and were putting more emphasis on individual visits, because they had a lot of very intelligent students that lacked communication skills. A veterinarian has to be able to communicate with farmers, ranchers, and pet owners. A high school transcript cannot tell an admissions officer if a student has strong communication skills. An individual visit can.

Do your homework. Your generation is very lucky because of the internet. You can quickly learn about anything. Go online and do research on the campus. Use the college navigator website that I used to produce the tables in regard to college costs and graduation rates. You will find a lot of great information there. Find out what the school is known for, unique alumni, and special programs. Remember, you are planning to live there for four years, so make sure you truly understand as much as you can about the school that way you will have something to talk about on the visit. The following site is the best place to start gathering information:

http://nces.ed.gov/collegenavigator/

> **The following are pieces of information that I believe are not important:**

Faculty-student ratio. The bigger the school the more deceptive these numbers are because graduate courses are traditionally used in the computation. The first year of college is the hardest because it is such an adjustment from high school. As mentioned before, a better question would be:

How big is your largest class on campus?

Percent of students receiving financial aid. Every family is different and most schools have their own unique make-up. Some schools attract wealthier families, so obviously less students receive financial aid. Some schools are way more expensive, so obviously a higher percent of students will receive financial aid. I don't care. I just need to know how much **free** money (grants and scholarships) a school will give my student.

Size of financial aid packages. This goes with the previous. Students from wealthy families need less money. More prestigious schools may have more money to hand out to students. Schools that attract better students most likely have students coming with outside scholarships.

Again, I don't care. I just need to know how much **free** money (grants and scholarships) a school will give my student.

The following are pieces of information that I believe are important to get before going on a visit:

Total costs from each of the previous four years. The website mentioned above will provide this information. Look at the percent increase from year to year and assume it will continue during the next four years.

Most recent four year graduation rate. Unfortunately, most schools skew their graduation rates, which is why you need to look it up. One fall a student visited a private university and was told by a young admissions officer that the school's four-year graduation rate was 95 percent (her dad also confirmed that was the number shared). I then told them to go to the website previously mentioned to get the actual rate which turned out to be 49 percent. They were shocked and the school was immediately eliminated from her list!

Number of undergraduate students enrolled. The more undergraduate students a school has, the bigger the general education classes will be.

Number of graduate students enrolled. The more graduate students a school has, the more likely the best professors will not be teaching undergraduate courses with reasonable class sizes. However, the more graduate students also means more research opportunities available on campus.

Retention rate. If most students are returning for their second year then that is good. If an unusual amount of students are not returning then that should be a red flag.

Placement rate from each of the previous four years. Notice I stated each of the previous four years.

One year I had a young lady who earned an ACT composite of 35, had straight A's, and attended numerous engineering summer camps around the country. This girl had an impressive resume. During one college visit, a school official boasted that the university's placement rate within six months of graduation was 93 percent. The girl's mom then asked two great questions (I need to add that this was all happening in an auditorium filled with about 200 parents and students):

1. **How many years were used in the computation?**

2. **What was the placement rate LAST YEAR?**

This caught the admissions official off guard. She said she was not sure but that she would get back to her with an answer within the week. The mom made sure to write down the questions and her email in order to make sure she did in fact receive the answers. As promised, the official responded.

Answer #1: The 93 percent placement rate went back to 1983.

Answer #2: Last year's placement rate was approximately 60%.

You need to know that "last year" referred to those that graduated in May of 2008, the beginning of the Great Recession. We are still in a volatile economy. Placement rates in the 80's and 90's don't mean much to current college graduates as we have already discussed. However, my real point is the following:

How many parents across the country just accept every statistic a college gives them as Gospel truth and never take the time to inquire how the numbers are computed as this mom did?

This leads to a very important point. Many presenters on college visits share statistics that they were simply given. They may not actually understand them or know how they were derived. Don't be afraid to ask questions. You want to make sure you are getting correct information.

I would encourage all parents to carefully learn about the university's career centers. For example at the University of Illinois, not only is there a career center for the whole university, but for individual colleges. The college of business strives to have a 100% placement rate and in 2012-2013 had a 93% employment rate as of January 14th, 2014.[19] Certain departments at certain schools have a stronger support network than others.

Have questions to ask. Visiting a school can be intimidating and overwhelming. A few years ago a bright young girl in my ACT classes was going on her first college visit and already had meetings set-up with various campus officials. However, she was not sure what to ask and wondered if I would be willing to produce a list of questions. I did and you will find those in the next section. I believe as you read through those questions you will understand why they are listed. If not, email me. If you have suggestions on additional questions, please email me. I want this information to help as many students and families as possible.

WARNING: Toward the end of every meeting it is common for the admissions officer to ask, "Do you have any questions?" Do not pull out the list and start by, asking, "Okay, question #1, what is your favorite color?" The point of the list is to help students get into a conversation with the admissions officer. The student will get better at this with practice.

NOTE: Students and parents should be reading this book. If your student is not reading this book, then at least have them read this section. High school students can sometimes overestimate their abilities and think they don't need to practice for certain things like a college visit. That's a problem. Even the most confident, self-assured high school senior can get overwhelmed on a college visit, especially when on a small group tour with other highly talented students who did take the time to prepare for the visit. There are no negatives to preparing for a visit.

Practice. Practicing prior to visiting a school is a great way to relax. Have a parent or another adult ask you possible questions. Practice the correct way to shake hands and practice making eye contact. Make sure your sitting posture is appropriate. Leave your cell phone in the car, so you will not be tempted to check it, especially in front of a college official (that's rude). In a very real sense this is a job interview.

Start Close. Visit schools close to your home first. Even better, visit a community college first. These visits tend to be less stressful and will give you a good feel of what to expect from a college admissions officer.

You will make mistakes on each visit and you will learn something new on each visit. The more visits you do, the more productive your visits will become, which is why you don't want to start with out-of-state schools.

Susan was one my ACT students. She always wanted to go to the University of Iowa. That was her dream school. The summer before her senior year, Susan and her mom planned a four-day trip to Iowa. Susan was so excited! When they got there, everything went wrong on Susan's part; she was really nervous, too emotional, and kept getting upset when things did not work out the way she had imagined.

During the four-hour drive home, Susan and her mom argued, cried, stopped talking, and then repeated the cycle. When Susan shared all of this information with me a week later, she began to cry again. She had a horrible experience. Her dream school became a nightmare and Iowa was crossed off her list.

I want to point out that Iowa did nothing wrong. Susan's mom confirmed that. Susan was just too nervous and not ready for the visit. Susan's story illustrates the importance of practicing close to home first and then as the student becomes more comfortable with the process move on to schools that are farther away. You do not have as many chances to visit an out-of-state school. A school close to home you can visit numerous times, so making a mistake is not as fatal.

Visuals. You need to take the following items to an individual visit.

- A copy of your high school transcript

- Your best letter of recommendation

- Your resume portfolio

This will provide the admissions officer an opportunity to quickly look at your transcript and ask any questions that may immediately come up. This also provides the student an opportunity to explain anything unusual. I had a junior in my spring semester ACT classes who unfortunately got mono. Not only was she unable to finish my class, but she missed a lot of school which affected her grades. Once she recovered and school was over, I allowed her to make up the entire class during my June crash course.

One weekend she was going to Iowa State University for an individual visit. I suggested that she take a copy of her high school transcript in order to explain what happened during the spring of her junior year when she was sick. After the weekend trip, she sent me an email to thank me for the suggestion. She said the admissions officer was very impressed that she brought a copy of her high school transcript and they reviewed it with her right then and there. Little things make a big difference.

The letter of recommendation will not be read in front of you, but there is a good chance it will be read later in the day and mean more because now they have a face with your name. If you only take one, then it most likely will be read. If you take more than one, then most likely they will be moved immediately to your student file.

I cannot tell you how many students have shared with me how admissions officers were impressed with their resume portfolio. It can really help get an individual meeting started in the right direction. A student comes into the office, smiles, looks the official right in the eyes, gives a firm handshake, and then says this is for you while handing the official the resume portfolio and LOR. Because the resume portfolio includes pictures and brief summaries, it's very easy for the official to glance at it and ask immediate questions, which helps eliminate any potential tension in the student.

If you are visiting schools during your junior year or early summer immediately after your junior year, then you most likely will not have your resume portfolio or LOR. That's not a problem. Once you have them, simply mail them to your "advocate" at the schools you have already visited. This will serve as a great reminder to them of the following:

"This is a reminder that we have met before,
and this is what I look like in case you had forgotten.

I also wanted to share what I have accomplished,
and to remind you that I really want to attend your school".

Again, little things can make a big difference.

What is the best way to discuss scholarships with the schools (cut through the college boiler plate and get to the core of the program's scholarship availability)?

This is where visiting schools early becomes important because it allows the student and parents to establish a relationship with someone in the admissions office. A few years ago, one of my ACT parents was taking a group of students to visit Washington University in St. Louis. He asked the Director of Admissions what is one question that parents should ask but don't. Without hesitation she said,

"Parents don't ask for more money.
If they don't tell us, we assume they've got it covered."

I cannot tell you how many parents I have met who thought it was inappropriate to even discuss money with schools. I've met parents who thought that you can't ask for more money. I've had conversations with parents who thought admissions officers could not help so why ask. The vast majority of parents in the country think this way.

Colleges need parents to think this way because these are the parents that encourage their student to accept a scholarship package without asking for more or simply encourage their student to attend a college after being accepted without asking for a scholarship. Don't be those families! If you are, you may lose out on thousands of dollars simply because you didn't ask a few questions.

> **IMPORTANT:** Never forget that the ability to negotiate with a school will depend on the student's academic record, personal statements, essays, letters of recommendations, references, and MOST IMPORTANTLY the student's ability to personally sell themselves to the college.

Chapter 17

College Visit Questions

IMPORTANT: I suggest that you ask each person you meet the following:

1. Where are they originally from?

2. How did they arrive at the university?

3. How long they have been at the university?

4. What do they like about the university?

It is human nature to want to talk about oneself. However, these individuals are used to talking about other people. For them, it will be a nice break from what they are accustomed to AND you will most likely get more honest and candid responses to your other questions.

Remember, you are interviewing them as much as they are interviewing you!

You do not have to ask all of these questions. These are just ideas to get you started.

Admissions Officer:

1. How many students typically apply to the college/university?

2. What percent of applicants are admitted?

3. What percent of the freshmen class return for their sophomore year?

4. What percent of the students graduate in FOUR years?

5. Why do some students take longer than four years?

6. What percent of the graduating class got jobs in their actual field of study?

7. What percent of the graduating class that applied to graduate schools got in?

8. What are things typical freshmen struggle with their first year?

9. What does your university base academic (merit) scholarships on and how are different financial levels determined?

10. What honors programs are available?

11. What work study programs are available?

12. When a high school senior selects your university, what happens next? (course selection, entrance exams, dorm selection/roommate pairing, summer freshmen orientation, etc.)

13. What services will the university supply to college graduates? (job placement, career center, etc.)

14. What makes your university unique compared to others in the state/region?

15. How is the relationship between the university and community? (Internships, community service, etc.)

16. Would it be possible to meet with a student in my particular field of interest that is a senior?

If possible, it would be fantastic if your family could take a senior student out to lunch (early dinner) to have a candid conversation about the university like Lisa did in the earlier story. If you can at least make a contact like this, then stay in communication with them the following weeks. This will help you receive a student's perspective on some of the above questions.

Professor/Dean:

1. How many students are in the college/department?

2. How many females? How many males?

3. What is the faculty – student ratio? (This can vary from department to department which is why I don't suggest asking the admissions officer.)

4. What is the typical class size for each year: freshmen, sophomore, junior, and senior? (For example, at the U of I classes, the sizes are very big the first two years but get smaller as the courses get more specific.)

5. What special programs does the college/department offer?

6. What internships are available and at what levels? (For example, are their work opportunities from younger students the summer between freshmen and sophomore years?)

7. How available are professors during the week to meet with students?

8. If I would come to your university, are they any particular courses that you highly recommend?

Student Tour Guide:

1. What did you first notice about this university when you arrived on campus?

2. What surprised you about the university that you were not aware of before you came?

3. Do you ever go meet with professors outside of class?

4. What are your thoughts on the dorms? Do many older students live off campus? What other living options are available?

5. How is transportation? How important is having a car on campus?

6. What does the community offer?

7. Have you, or a group of students, ever had lunch/dinner with a professor?

8. Are study groups common on campus?

9. What internships are available?

10. What work opportunities are available? (part-time jobs, etc.)

11. What makes the school special?

12. What would you like to see changed at the school?

13. What don't you like about the school? Do you think most people have the same sentiment?

Student tour guides are selected for specific reasons as well as availability. These guides tend to be very positive and have great communication skills. The above questions should help give you an idea whether or not this particular tour guide will be helpful. A tour guide may or may not have your interests, academic goals, or personality which will determine how helpful they will be to you in regard to getting specific information.

This is why you want to meet with a student in your particular field of interest. For example, if a student is interested in becoming a teacher, an education major is going to much more knowledgeable about the above. Ask that college student similar questions as the professor and student tour guide.

Chapter 18

The Basic Timeline

What courses does a student need to take in order to be college ready?

Actual requirements can vary from college to college and degree program to degree program. For example, engineering majors are going to have much higher requirements in certain subjects like math and science than a typical liberal arts student. The following is a basic framework to follow in order to provide a strong academic foundation for college and meet any special requirements a college might have:

- *4 years of Mathematics*
- *4 years of English*
- *4 years of Physical Sciences including Biology, Chemistry, and Physics*
- *4 years of History*
- *3 years of Foreign Language*

Taking less than three years of Foreign Language in high school may require a student to take a foreign language class in college. College foreign language courses tend to be much harder than high school foreign language classes.

Avoid easier Social Studies courses such as psychology and sociology. At many high schools they are considered easy As but tend not to develop the academic skills necessary to be competitive in college.

I will take a moment to set-up a basic timeline assuming the student is just finishing up their sophomore year. These steps are written to the student, hence the verbiage used.

1. Take ACT in June right after your sophomore year to see where you rank nationally and get a copy of your test information release.

2. Visit your closest community college in order to practice a campus visit. This would also be an ideal time to learn how you can start taking college courses through their college.

3. Take my summer ACT class either live or the online video class to learn how to be a better test performer. This will not only better prepare you for the ACT, but it will help you with high school tests. The junior year is a lot harder than the first two years of high school.

4. Visit 2 or 3 universities that are in the area before your junior year starts. This will give you a better feel for what a college visit is like and will help you start getting motivated academically for your upcoming junior year.

EMAIL: Skepticism turned to Confidence

Mr. Franklin, thank you so much for providing me with the confidence I needed for preparing for and taking the ACT. I must admit that I was skeptical about how much taking your classes would actually help me. After taking all 14 sessions, I am pleased to say that I was amazed and impressed, to say the very least. I would also like to thank you for providing further advice outside of your paid responsibilities. It definitely shows that you truly do care about the success of each and every one of your students.

Chris

5. Take the September or October ACT to see how much you have improved since the June ACT.

6. Take the December ACT in order to be able to get a copy of the test information release.

7. Visit two schools in the spring of your junior year in order to increase academic motivation.

8. Take the National April ACT in order to re-evaluate your national ranking and order a copy of your test information release.

9. Get a copy of your high school transcript at the end of your junior year. Know what is on it.

10. Before your junior year ends, ask the BEST English teacher in your school if they would be willing to review your personal statement during the summer. Remember to get their **summer**

email address (not all teachers check their school email address during the summer).

11. Take the ACT again in June unless you have earned a 32+. Every point makes a difference.

12. Write essays and personal statements and have drafts completed prior to start of school. This would also be an ideal time to work with a professional editor if wanting help right from the beginning.

13. Visit schools during the summer and attempt to have all first visits completed by August 1st.

14. If you have a good feel for any particular schools, attempt to make a second visit in August or early fall when college is in session. This provides you an opportunity to meet students and see the school in a different light.

15. During the first week of school ask the BEST English teacher to review your final summer drafts. I would also have a professional editor review your drafts before finalizing them.

16. Come August begin filling out college applications.

17. Keep in touch with each school contact (your advocate) through every step of the process.

18. Get 10 letters of recommendations with the goal of having 10 copies by September 1st.

19. Before sending in your college application, reach out to your school advocate. Sometimes they will ask you to send it directly to them. Most deadlines are November 1st/December 1st.

20. Ask about any honors programs or scholarship interviews you may be eligible for. Be aware of any details associated with those programs.

21. If you are eligible for a special scholarship or honors program, then see if you can meet with the person in charge of the program in order to learn about the process before you are required to go through it.

22. When acceptance letters and scholarship packages arrive, begin re-evaluating your position.

23. Meet with your top choices and ask for more money (assuming an academic scholarship was received).

Chapter 19

Patience

Troy scored a 35 on his ACT early in his junior year, which allowed him to start the college process sooner than most. His top choice was Washington University in St. Louis. Troy was a straight A student with a great ACT score, so he did not think it was necessary to do an individual visit to Wash U, so he visited during one of those big weekends where he walked around campus with many other students.

During the fall of his senior year, he was not accepted by Wash U and was asked if he would like to be put on the wait list. He was upset and declined the wait list offer. He eventually decided to go to Illinois Wesleyan University and play soccer.

On May 5th of Troy's senior year the phone rang and the Wash U admissions office was on the other line. It was during the school day,

216

so Troy's mom answered the phone. Wash U told her that they were going through their wait list and wanted to know if Troy would be interested in considering Wash U. Troy's mom was confused, because Troy declined to be put on the wait list. Troy's mom thanked Wash U for calling but explained that he had already decided to go to IWU, which had offered him a $96,000 scholarship. The Wash U admissions officer paused for a moment and then said,

"Would he consider Wash U if we gave him $100,000?"

On May 10th Troy's family went down to visit Wash U. On May 12th he accepted Wash U's invitation and scholarship offer. That same day Troy contacted IWU to inform them of his decision to go to Wash U instead and IWU graciously accepted Troy's decision.

Where did Wash U get $100,000 to offer to a student they initially deemed unworthy of admissions in the first place?

Many schools require students to make decisions about acceptance and academic scholarships by May 1st. Assume for a moment that Jill gets accepted to five colleges and each offer her an academic scholarship. Jill can only attend one college, so as soon as she makes a decision she informs the other four that she is declining their invitation. Jill's decision allows those four other colleges to take Jill's scholarship offer and award it to another student that has not accepted yet.

Apparently, Wash U had a lot of scholarship offers that were not accepted that particular school year by May 1st leading to an incoming freshmen class that would be too small. Apparently Wash U worked their way through their wait list but still did not have enough incoming freshmen, so they began looking at students like Troy that declined an offer to be on the wait list.

This was mentioned earlier in the book but I will repeat this very important point: regardless of when a student decides on a college they still cannot begin college until late August after their high school graduation. Encourage your student to be patient. I have had many academically strong students get their scholarship packages increased dramatically during the month of April as May 1st crept closer.

Chapter 20

Putting It All Together

One of my former ACT students, Lauren, serves as the perfect example of putting everything I have shared together in order to have a successful journey through the college selection process.

Lauren began her ACT preparation during the summer between her sophomore and junior year of high school. She continued during the spring semester of her junior year, and then again during my June ACT Test Prep Crash Course immediately after her junior year. She took the test early and often in order to see where she was at, made adjustments along the way, and continued to prepare in order to maximize her score. She made great strides which included improving seven points on the ACT math test. Her final ACT composite was a 25.

Lauren's family attended the parent seminar offered in the summer after her junior year in order to make sure they were aware of new information that would help their daughter find the right school.

Because Lauren had already taken my ACT classes, she had learned the importance of visiting schools early. Before her senior year began, she had already visited all the schools on her list multiple times and knew her contacts at each school very well.

Lauren's essays, personal statement, and visits included specific details about one major area of her life: writing a book. She was looking for a college that would help advance her ability to continue writing in the future.

After each visit Lauren followed up with personal contacts, thank you cards, emails with questions and updates, and phone calls when appropriate. Lauren kept her top choices constantly updated about her book, which was still in the process of being self-published during the time she was visiting schools. When Lauren received a PDF file of the book cover, she shared it with her contacts. When the book was put up on Amazon, she made sure they were emailed a link. When she obtained hard copies, she sent one to each of her contacts.

I had students ask me why was she doing all of that? It's very simple. Each time she reached out, she reminded each school who she was and the book connection made it much easier for them to remember her. Realize that most college admissions officers are meeting thousands of high school students and parents each year. It's a challenge to remember everyone. It is your responsibility to help them remember you.

Lauren's top choice offered her a $36,000 scholarship in the fall of her senior year. Notice I gave very little details about her academic record. She was a good student which made it easier for the school to award her the scholarship, but that's not the only reason she earned it.

Lauren demonstrated that she was different, that she was not the typical high school student. When colleges talk about wanting diversity on campus, most people think ethnicity. That is small part of having a diverse campus. Colleges mean students who have had different experiences for a wide variety of reasons. Many factors can create diversity. The following is a list that is certainly not all inclusive.

General	Brief Example
Ethnicity	Student is Hispanic.
Socio-Economic Status	Student grew up poor.
Immigrant	Family moved from India. Student had to adjust to new culture.
Geographic	Student grew up in Alaska.
Schooling	Student was home schooled.
Work	Student started own lawn mowing business and employed friends.
Physical Limit	Student was born without a hand and made the volleyball team.
Learning Disability	Student with Dyslexia scored a 29 on the ACT and excels in school.
Accomplishments	Student wrote a book and got it self-published her senior year.

You will not necessarily know what a college or university will be looking for in regard to potential students, so don't worry. Too many families attempt to figure it out in order to "beat the system." Students will be encouraged to do things simply to enhance their college application and more often than not that approach fails.

Lauren didn't write a book to impress a college. She wants to be a writer. She had a story to tell, she started writing it, got help from teachers, learned about the publishing business world, ran into some roadblocks, made adjustments, and began studying business in order to learn how to promote her book. This is what she wants to do in her life at this time. She simply made sure every school knew the real Lauren.

In the spring of Lauren's senior year, she had a book signing event at the local Barnes & Noble. I found out about it because of an article in the local newspaper. I took my daughters to meet Lauren and to get signed copies for the family to read. Lauren's mom and I spoke for a while about many things, in particular how this journey with the book had changed Lauren into a much more confident young lady with a clear focus.

Lauren used to be very shy and quiet. However, the book brought out her passion. Lauren made arrangements her senior year to have a free class period, so she could continue her work with her writing which included a draft for another book as well as promoting the one just published. She contacted the local newspaper about the upcoming book signing. The paper was so impressed that they decided to do the story about her PRIOR to the book signing. In short, she received a lot of free publicity and all of her books in the store were sold within one hour of her book signing (it was scheduled for three hours). She also had been invited to speak to various high school classes about her experience in writing a book. All of this from a girl who used to be afraid to speak up in class.

What does this have to do with your student?

First, parents, help your student re-examine their life. Assist them in realizing what events changed them, challenges they faced and how they overcame those challenges. I have learned over the years that this is very difficult for high school students, especially hard-working students. Colleges, employers, and people in general admire someone who shows direction, leadership, takes initiative, and follows through. Work ethic is an indicator that people don't always talk about, but they do look for it.

- For Emily, it was a mission's trip.

- For Lexi, it was my math class.

- For Lauren, it was writing a book.

Second, and this is the most important and final point of this book, Lauren did not need college to find her immediate focus or figure out what she would like to do and neither does your student. College is simply a tool, a stepping stone, a few years in one's life where a lot of growing up takes place before the student enters the next phase: ADULT LIFE IN THE REAL WORLD.

Keep college in perspective. It's not the end. For many, it's just one small part of the beginning of becoming an adult.

Lauren gave me permission to share her personal statement that was submitted with her college applications. You will find it on the next page. It serves as another good example of the importance of focusing on one event.

A dream. When young, we dream of being doctors, dancers, or firefighters. In third grade, I dreamed of being an author. I wanted to share a story with the world. A story that would make people laugh and cry. A story people would remember—a story for which would be remembered.

In seventh grade I told my parents I was going to write and publish a novel. They reacted like any parents would, "That sounds great dear." Not losing hope, I began my novel. Six chapters in I hit a wall; I had brought so many elements into the story that there was no climbing that wall. Eighth grade brought a new story and a new start. With my book flourishing, high school started and my book stopped as sports, new responsibilities, and priorities arose.

A creative writing class during my sophomore year became a turning point as I established the discipline of writing every day. With my amazing teacher, Mr. Yanchus to guide me, my evolving novel really took off. To my sheer disappointment, my creative writing teacher—my mentor—retired. Fortunately, my new creative writing teacher and I clicked. With her encouragement, my story was completed during the fall of my junior year.

With a completed story, neither my teacher nor I knew precisely what to do next. Finishing an exhaustive edit of my story, I began to research how to publish a book. We weighed the pros and cons of agent-based traditional publishing versus self-publishing. Internet searches were informative and lead to books describing the how to and the who does of the publishing world. They included the process to follow, costs, and warnings about scams.

Heeding their advice, I submitted my manuscript electronically for copyright. I chose my top pick to publish and reached an agreement. I shipped my manuscript off along with cover concepts, as I was to receive two or three options for my cover. My first cover design arrived a few days later, as an over the top girly pink cover. Understand this is not a romance novel: it's a story about a fight and struggle to stay alive while everyone you know is missing or gone. A pink cover was not going to do it. Reneging on our agreement the publisher declined to redo the cover. It was a difficult, but important, lesson to learn. This is a business and I needed to be professional throughout all my decisions no matter how challenging those decisions may be.

Reviewing my research led me to another seemingly credible option: Dog Ear Publishing. They were high on my list and had a local office. I was offered the opportunity to visit their company and meet with my author representative. After the meeting and learning from my previous experience, I was confident this company would be a better fit for me and my novel. Thus far, I have been very pleased with their services and would recommend them whole-heartedly to other self-publishing authors.

My novel is now in the hands of professionals. So that's the end of it right? There is another aspect. How will your work be marketed? Today we are all in touch globally via tweets, texts, email, and YouTube videos. We are marketed to in a volume and manor like no other. As young people, we are evolving new ways every day to be seen. There are so many opportunities and ways to put yourself and your products in front of people. Learning about marketing especially at such a young age has taught me so much. I have realized that marketing is something I want to pursue thanks to the amazing journey I am currently on with my first self-published novel.

Self-publishing means you have to sell your own novel. You are the marketer, the advertiser, the main and only account executive. Students at school look at me strangely when they see me reading marketing, publishing, and business books or magazine articles about those very topics. That's okay because learning something for a grade is not nearly as powerful as learning for life. I have learned and endured many new things on this incredible journey.

Honestly, if my novel never becomes a major commercial success it will not matter, because it has already been a personal success and continues to lead me to other areas, like marketing, which I never thought I would go. Now I look toward college to increase my knowledge, understanding of application, and opportunity towards my future goals.

Chapter 21

End Game: Olivia's Story

Olivia is one of my former ACT prep students. When she was only a junior in high school, I could tell she was wise beyond her years. This is her story.

Olivia graduated from Peoria Christian High School, one of the top private schools in the State of Illinois. She had a 3.86 grade point average and earned a 29 on her ACT. As a high school senior, Olivia was presented with Service Above Self Award and scholarship through the Peoria North Rotary Club.

Olivia applied to the University of Illinois, Bradley University, Drake University, and Butler University. She was accepted to all four schools. Olivia went on to the University of Illinois to study English but after two years changed her major to Communications with a minor in

Business. Despite the national trend of college students taking six years to earn an undergraduate degree, Olivia is graduating a year early. I recently asked her to share how she was able to graduate early from one of the top universities in the country.

What did you do in order to finish a year early?

To be honest, graduating early was not in my initial plan going into my college freshman year. In high school, I took a dual credit biology class (4 credit hours). I also received AP English credits (4 credit hours) and due to a high enough ACT English score, I was exempt from another entry level college rhetoric class (3 credit hours). So, I had received 11 hours in college credits before my freshman year even started.

The following summer, I took 7 hours of math courses at Illinois Central College. It was then that I fully realized how ahead I was and decided to pursue graduating early. This past summer, I took an online course through the U of I and I also received credit for an internship I had; together, those both totaled 6 hours. I have taken regular course loads each semester at U of I. The most hours I took in one semester were 19, and the least hours I took in one semester were 12. I average about 16 credit hours per semester.

Why did you decide to finish a year early?

I decided to finish a year early largely for financial reasons. A majority of the cost of my schooling is being paid for via student loans. While my parents will help me, I realized the person responsible for paying a majority of those back someday was me. Honestly, my academic advisor at U of I was not in favor of the idea. She planned out my schedules to take 12 hours simply so I would finish in 4 years. She told me not to take summer courses. As I was already ahead of the game, I thought it would be silly to take light course loads solely for the reason of prolonging my time at college. For me, graduating early was the obvious choice.

Do you feel like you are missing out on anything in regard to the college experience by graduating a year early?

Truthfully, I do sometimes feel as if I will be missing out by graduating early. I will certainly miss my friends and the life I have made for myself in Champaign. I'm a little scared, too! All I have known how to do my whole life is be a student and I often wonder if I have enough experience for the "real world" work force. Despite this, I am still confident graduating early is the right decision. The financial benefit far outweighs the social costs. While the thought of working is intimidating at times, I look at graduating early as giving myself an extra year to gain experience and explore what the work force has to offer.

Olivia did almost everything we have suggested in this book:

1. She took a dual credit course and earned four college credits while in high school.

2. She took the AP English test and earned four college credits while in high school.

3. She prepared for the ACT and scored so high on one of the subject tests that she earned three college credits while in high school.

4. The summer after her freshman year of college she earned seven college credits at her local community college.

5. She averaged over the 15 credit hours necessary to earn an undergraduate degree in four years.

6. Because she did so much course work outside of the traditional school year, she could have lightened her course load to 12 credit hours per semester in order to graduate in four years.

7. She was aware of the financial advantages of graduating early.

8. She understands that she is primarily responsible for paying back her student loans, not her parents.

9. She understood that there are actual social costs to enjoying a college experience for another year.

10. She realizes that graduating early from college will give her an extra year of real world experience in the work force. Something that is not gained during the college years.

This book is how to prepare, pick, and pay less for college in this century. You are reading this book because you have a student that will soon be going to college. Olivia's story represents the end as well as the real beginning. As mentioned in the beginning of the book, college represents a very small time in an individual's life. College is a stepping stone. Help your student keep it all in perspective and may they, like Olivia, end their college years as a success ready to enter the next phase of life.

Bonus Material

The following sections include responses to submitted questions that are relevant but could not fit in previous sections.

Is it worth it?

We will have two kids in college at the same time in a few years. Will the money being spent on college be worth it?

I have six kids and I appreciate the importance of this question. College is supposed to be four years of mind training not job training, and this is where the problem arises. People misinterpret statistics that "show" college graduates make more money than those who do not graduate from college. That's misleading. People who choose to attend college and persevere during those four years tend to have more natural abilities and stronger work ethic. However, that's not all college students. There are also a lot of talented individuals who have fantastic work ethic that do not attend college or end up dropping out when they realize college is not preparing them for what they want to do (think Bill Gates and Steve Jobs – both college dropouts).

Talk to college graduates who are 40+ years old. Ask them what knowledge was gained in an undergraduate college course that specifically helps them now in their job. Most cannot think of anything, some will come up with something, and a small few can honestly claim that actual courses had a direct correlation to their current employment. However, people 40+ years old most likely went to college when it cost a lot less, so it most likely was worth it. Now, let's fast forward to today.

Is it worth going to college and spending $100K for one student? Is it worth a student beginning life in their early 20s with a $50K college loan, a $5K credit card debt, and a $10K car loan? Don't forget any potential loans that parents may need to take on. This young college graduate may also want to get married to someone they met in college who has the exact same loans. Congratulations! This young couple now gets to start life with over $130K in debt and most likely will want to get a house but can't because of all of the debt they have already amassed before the age of 22 years old. Welcome to life for many young college graduates in the 21st Century.

Let's not mislead young people into thinking college will give them a better life because it does not. A college provides nothing except opportunities. It's up to a student to take advantage of various opportunities. College is a financial risk. There is no guarantee of financial return (remember, OCCUPY WALL STREET which was made up primarily of young college graduates who were unemployed and were already struggling to pay back their college loans).

The financial risk grows when the student "invests" more into the education. This is really where parents can help their student. What is the purpose of your automobile? I'm being serious. People view cars differently. Personally, I need a reliable vehicle to get around. Others feel the need to spend a lot of money on cars to increase their self-esteem. These different goals lead to different "investments." I can spend $15,000 to get a good reliable vehicle that will give me 250,000+ miles. I know many young people who have invested over $50,000 in vehicles while still living with their parents. You have to decide what "worth" is.

A home is no different. During this recent recession in the community where I live, I have seen young college educated couples with no kids buy homes that were too big and too expensive only to be forced to sell at a tremendous loss due to a recent job loss suffered by one of the spouses.

College is no different. There are ways to lower costs: start taking college courses before graduating from high school, take advantage of community colleges, stay close to home, live close to home, pick a major that provides more flexibility in the real world, graduate in four years, and work during college in order to reduce the need for college loans.

EMAIL: 7 point jump in ACT score allows Amy to opt out of college courses (saving her money)!

Jason,

Your ACT class not only helped me with my actual ACT, but your tips helped me with my PSAE as well. My first ACT was a 19, but after taking all four of your courses I didn't feel nervous about taking the test at all, I actually felt confident. My composite score for my ACT was a 26! Thank you!

I plan on going to Lincoln Land Community College and enrolling in their nursing program. Since my ACT scores were high enough, I am able to opt out of some of the general education courses and opt in to the classes I need for my Associates Degree in Nursing. I still have not received any scholarship information, but things are looking up!

Thank you so much for all your help!
Amy

Misguided Mindset

The following are questions parents submitted that require a very candid response because they reveal that there are parents who need to change their mindset in regard to how they view college for their student. I do not want parents to be misguided because that will lead to students being misguided.

How do you select a great college that will ensure a great job/career if your kid does not know what she wants to major in?

No college can ensure a great job or career. If you visit a school that tells you this, then eliminate them from the list. They are being dishonest and if they are misleading you on this then they potentially are giving your misinformation about other things.

Most colleges and universities have career centers to help students with resumes and finding jobs. However, they are simply tools nothing more. It's a college graduate's responsibility to find a job, not anyone else's and that's a fact of life. Right now, there are a lot of recent college graduates who are unemployed or underemployed. I'm sure many were told that the college would ensure them a job in their field of study. They got burned by a false image. Don't let the same happen to your student.

How to determine which school provides the best academic assistance?

When a student gets into college there is NO ONE holding their hand anymore except in some circumstances their parents. Succeeding in college is about a student taking initiative. Students aren't forced to go to office hours or even class. There is no detention; the only penalties a student MAY receive is academic failure (and getting kicked out and sent home from class if you are disruptive or late).

People won't go out of their way to help a student find academic assistance. If a student wants help they will have to seek it out themselves. There are many avenues to gain help. Many departments offer free student tutors. Teaching assistants tend to be available at bigger schools and are always there to help, and even professors for smaller classes. There are learning specialists at almost all schools, but they generally will not seek out a student; the student will have to seek them out. This is an example of how college is a step into the real world - no one is holding the student's hand anymore.

Community colleges offer a lot of academic assistance programs because most community college students were not necessarily strong high school students; therefore, they never developed the necessary academic work ethic to succeed at the college level.

Almost all four-year universities now offer study skills courses, workshops, and seminars to help students, especially first-year college students. Some colleges even require freshmen to take these courses. Many schools also have special assistance programs for students with learning disabilities. If your student has a learning disability, then make sure to ask about assistance programs when visiting schools.

> **WARNING:** Do not assume the college knows your student has a learning disability. This should be discussed in detail with college officials on an individual visit. Do not assume the school will automatically put your student in special programs designed for college students with LD. Be proactive and follow up with the school to make sure everything is in order.

Do volunteer activities help, what looks good in the student's application, do sports help, etc.?

This is a great question because there is so much misinformation passed around high schools about this topic. I had a student who played a very unusual instrument in an orchestra. It was so unique that I cannot even remember the name of it. She had just come from a lesson, so I asked her a few questions before class started. I learned that she started lessons in fifth grade and she HATED it! I asked her why she kept playing since she disliked it so much. Her mom told her that playing a rare instrument would look good on her college application.

I had another student who ran cross country because his guidance counselor told him that individual sports look good on a college application. I had another student who was involved in over twenty activities because her guidance counselor told her the more activities the better. Another student did a lot of "volunteer" work because his parents forced him in order to enhance his college application.

What lesson does this teach young people? Do things to simply look good. That's what politicians do which is why national surveys show that politicians are the least trusted professional group. Colleges are not fooled. They know the above happens; therefore, the school gives little weight to extra-curricular activities simply listed on the college application. This is where essays, personal statements, and meetings become very important.

IMPORTANT: You want to encourage your student to do activities that will allow them to grow as a person, not because you think it might look good on a college application. If the student is truly engaged in the activity then they will be passionate about it and want to share their zeal with others. When a student writes their essays and personal statements then they will have something to write about because it is important to them. When a student is meeting with college officials and these activities come up, then the student's real passion will come out and be on full display. That's real and that's what a college wants to see.

College admissions officers are some of the best people you will ever meet. They are very genuine and very receptive. They can easily tell when teenagers are being sincere as opposed to putting on a show.

My daughter needs to figure out what she wants to do. We are not interested in paying for an expensive school until she knows what she is doing.

Why would you pay for an expensive school even if she knew what she wanted to do? Did you buy your daughter an expensive car once she figured out how to drive? Would you encourage her to buy an expensive house once she got a job? Picking a college is the best time to teach financial and practical lessons to your child who will soon be an adult.

WARNING: If you do not teach your student financial lessons when picking a college, then down the road you may join the growing number of parents who have unemployed or underemployed college graduates living with them.

"Could not fit but good" Questions

The following were very specific questions submitted that I could not address earlier in the book but are valuable, so we decided to put them at the end. If you have read this book and there is something I did not answer, then please email your question to me at Jason.Franklin@BetterPrepSuccess.com. I'm here to help. If I don't know the answer, I will be honest and let you know.

What does a student need to do to audition and be accepted into the music program at the college of his choice?

I have had a few families go through this process, and I have learned that it is much different than the traditional application process. Most schools will overlook small deficiencies in an academic record if the student is truly talented. The music scholarships, like athletic scholarships, then become much more subjective than academic scholarships. If a student already knows what music program they are interested in, then they need to immediately contact those schools and find out how the audition process works because every school is different. The key is to contact them, speak to a live person in the music department, and ask them.

EMAIL: Melissa shares how she chose her college

Dear Jason,

I've already made my decision! I will be attending Illinois Wesleyan University in the fall for Music Education!

I had applied to three colleges: Indiana University, University of Illinois, and Illinois Wesleyan University. First of all, I never thought I would apply to Illinois or Illinois Wesleyan, but they were recommended by friends in the music field. I auditioned for IWU in early November, and I found in December that I not only got in, I received a $21,000 Alumni scholarship per year based on academics and my audition. That was a great Christmas present!

I wasn't sold yet, though. I had to record a pre-screening tape for Indiana in November, but I got the flu the night before I planned to record it. It was the sickest I have ever been, so we postponed the recording. However, I could barely talk a week later, let alone sing. When I did not get asked back for an audition, I wasn't too bummed. I actually took it as a sign that I was not meant to be there anyway.

Then, in January, I auditioned for the University of Illinois. I got in, but I did not receive scholarship. I really liked the big campus, I wanted to be in the Marching Illini, and I really liked some of the staff with whom I would be working. My heart was there for a very long time.

On the other hand, my head was telling me IWU, so I was very conflicted for a very long time. I thought that I would be struggling right up until the deadline. I did a lot of research between the two programs, and after lots of thought, I determined that the program at Illinois was not what I wanted. Still, I couldn't let go of the big campus atmosphere and the marching band.

I took one more trip to IWU with my chorus director (who also went there) for one of her previous student's senior recital, and I loved the atmosphere. Finally, my heart and my head matched. I sat with the decision for a week, and I never looked back. I had a lesson with a professor from Wesleyan over Spring Break, and he told me that if Illinois came back with any scholarship to call IWU admissions because they would help me out. He also said that he would personally write a note to them to let them know how special of a student I was and that the music department would benefit greatly from my talent. And that was it, how could I look back after that?

I just accepted two days ago, and I am officially an Illinois Wesleyan Titan! I am so excited to begin my college journey. Thank you again for such an awesome class!! It really helped me with my ACT score which I'm sure boosted my scholarship!

Sincerely,
Melissa

What colleges provide the greatest employment opportunities in the sciences at the best cost?

The only employment opportunities I am aware of that a college can provide are those in research. Therefore, a student would want to look at attending bigger universities that receive a large amount of funding for research. I have to be honest and share that these opportunities are very limited and highly competitive. Foreign students in particular flock to these particular schools.

> **WARNING:** The University of Michigan for decades has been one of the top places to go for research. However, look at what has happened to the State of Michigan since the Great Recession of 2008. As mentioned previously, make sure you get recent statistics on schools. A lot has changed in the last five or so years. Having said the above, Michigan still is a strong school and is still a desirable place to do research, but the issues in Detroit (as of this writing the city has officially declared bankruptcy) may spread to the rest of the state.

Our son is generally interested in Engineering (no specific field). Does he need to pick a college of engineering right away or just major in one of the physical sciences and steer toward engineering later?

There are certain majors that require a student to begin in that department and engineering is one of them. Engineering is rigorous. Some schools will not allow a student to transfer into an engineering program. It's better to start in engineering and then if the student wants to change majors, it will be a lot easier. If he elects not to declare his major upon entrance into college, make sure to be aware of and take any courses that a specific department (such as the school of Engineering) may require before a student can apply into that major.

Top tier schools can be very restrictive in regard to changing majors when the major is rigorous. For example, the University of Illinois Business School is highly selective, allowing in only about 200 applicants after May of their freshman year, with close to 90% of those students maintaining over a 3.5 GPA.[20]

How to determine which colleges have strongest information technology/computer programs, internship programs (school and summer), and employment placement assistance?

Ironically, the top information technology/computer leaders in the country did not come from universities but rather the top companies or self-training. Technology advances so fast that college curriculums are years behind. I have relatives that work in State Farm National Headquarters information technology divisions. I constantly hear stories that State Farm spends the first year training recent college graduates in order to catch them up with the real world.

If a student is very interested in information technology, then encourage them to seek out internship and work experience in these sectors. Recently, I had a high school junior in my ACT classes that was doing a paid internship at State Farm National Headquarters in information technology. It's a growing field that is constantly looking for young talent. I'm not suggesting that those interested in this field should not go to college. What I am saying is that this is a field that is constantly changing and real work experience is invaluable.

Are there any nursing employers that offer tuition assistance programs if you work for them during school?

Obamacare is dramatically changing the entire medical community. We know there is going to be a shortage of medical professionals at all levels. My aunt and cousin live in Louisville and got their schooling paid for by one of the city hospitals. Part of the arrangement was that they had to work so many years for the hospital upon graduation. That's guaranteed employment – even better.

The best thing to do is to contact schools and ask if they are aware of any such programs or contact medical centers and see if they offer such programs.

How to find possible college volleyball (sport) opportunities?

Annie Luhrsen assist families with the college sport recruiting process. She comes from a family of four kids and all four played Division I college sports. More importantly, she went through the recruiting process twice. I would strongly encourage anyone interested in playing college sports to visit BetterPrepSuccess.com to learn more about her recruiting seminar. The following is her short bio that is included in the seminar materials.

Annie Luhrsen
Coming out of high school, Annie was a two-time Illinois all-state selection and member of the 2008 USA Volleyball Junior National Team. She went on to play volleyball at the University of Connecticut where she had immediate success, was named BIG EAST Freshman of the Year, was first team all-conference, and was the Northeast Regional Freshman of the Year. She then transferred to the University of Illinois,

was the starting setter for the team that made it to the 2011 National Championship match, and was named to the NCAA All-Tournament team. Most would assume she simply transferred to the University of Illinois in order to play on a nationally ranked team; however, that is not the case.

Like many high school student-athletes, Annie was unfamiliar with how to navigate the recruiting process and made mistakes which led her to a school that was not the best fit for her. Despite her athletic success at UConn, she was not having a positive experience and was ready to walk away from college volleyball for good.

She decided to transfer and went through the college recruiting process again. This time she learned from her experiences and gained quality counsel from others. This eventually led to a more sound decision and a commitment to a school that was the best fit for her. Annie does not want others to go through what she did and is passionate about providing information to students – and their parents – that will help them not only succeed but also enjoy the college recruiting process.

EMAIL: Family gets to enjoy son's college sports experience

Jason – our son will be going to Illinois State University this fall and he was awarded a partial scholarship for football. We are very excited for him as ISU was always his college of choice and the chance to play football there as well was just the icing on the cake. We also like the fact that he will be close to home as well (parent speaking).

He really enjoyed your classes and we attended one of your parent seminars on picking and paying for college. It was exceptional and really helped us in the college selection process. We are always recommending your classes to others.

Best of luck to you! Thanks for helping all these students become better prepared for college!

Is it necessary to be in a pre-law undergraduate program or is another field of study more beneficial?

I have been told that if a student knows they are going to go on to graduate school in a specific field then it is best to be in a different undergraduate program. For example, history students will often go on to attend law school. Of course, there are exceptions. A student planning on attending medical school needs to be in an undergraduate program that will prepare them for medical school. The key is to ask the right people. In this case, I would talk to law schools and find out what they look for in an undergraduate student.

> **WARNING:** Beware of programs that streamline a student into the university's law school. The University of Illinois has the ILEAP program where a student applies while still an undergrad before the standard application process for the rest of the nation's law schools. The advantage is early acceptance and no need to submit an LSAT score. However, the disadvantage is that forces the top U of I students into committing to Illinois before even investigating and applying to other schools. This limits opportunities.

> **WARNING:** I would encourage anyone considering law school to investigate what has been recently happening to law school graduates. In short, law schools are producing too many graduates and there are not enough job opportunities associated with the law profession. This is the 21st Century, the world is changing, and it may become a profession that will not be as needed in the future. I point this out because law school is not cheap.

How do you reduce the costs for those schools (I have twins, does that help)?

It does help having siblings attend the same school. The smaller the school, the more important this may become. The stronger the students are, the better. One, colleges know that siblings attending the same school are more likely to graduate from that school. The job of the admissions office is to pick students they think will come and graduate in four years. Siblings assist each other emotionally. That's a big deal. Two, colleges understand that one family is attempting to finance multiple kids, so they may be able to come up with additional funds. Again, the stronger the students the better.

We are looking at medical school after undergraduate years, so looking to keep first four years to a debt minimum. Any thoughts?

Many believe that Obamacare when fully implemented will create a severe shortage of doctors, nurses, and other health professionals. This may work in your advantage. I suspect that in the very near future hospitals will pay for medical school for top students under the condition that they work for them for so many years once out of medical school.

Students who truly have the ability to go to medical school, should have a high school academic record that would allow them to get a major academic scholarship at non-top tier or top tier schools. I say this because most pre-med students want to go to top-tier schools and then on to medical school. Most believe they will eventually become wealthy doctors, so they will have no problem paying back college loans. Don't be fooled. Our national healthcare system is currently going through very dramatic changes that are unprecedented. The future impact on the medical profession is unclear.

We would like our daughter to stay in the Illinois system unless her potential major is not represented at Illinois universities (in order that we might capture the value of the 50% tuition remission). What do we need to know?

If a student has the 50 percent tuition then this provides a lot of flexibility. One, they already have a great deal. Two, this allows them to look for additional scholarships outside of the school or other schools, knowing they are already in financial great shape.

There is one catch to the 50 percent tuition deal: some schools may automatically eliminate the student from receiving additional scholarships. However, schools like ISU, will still allow the student to compete for additional scholarships. Make sure you have all of your facts straight about the program as rules may vary from school to school.

EMAIL: Nicole is getting paid to $2,000 to go to college!!!

Hi Jason!

I got your postcard in the mail the other day and realized I never updated you on my college search/selection process. I only applied at one school: Illinois State. I knew that was where I wanted to go. With my ACT (33), I knew I would be accepted to ISU, and I wasn't worried about paying for it since I had half price tuition. And although most people--like my counselor at school--thought I was a little crazy, it all worked out. Just a couple of weeks ago, I found out I received the Presidential Scholarship at ISU. They recently raised the value to $11,000 per year. Needless to say, I was thrilled.

Something perhaps a little unique about this scholarship is that it is towards cost of attendance, not just tuition. Since my father is employed at the university, I have half price tuition. This means that only $7,000 or so of my scholarship is used for tuition. The rest can be applied to books, fees, meal plans etc. Since I am intending to live at home, the school will be writing me a check for around $2,000 each year. In this day and age, I'm pretty sure this is practically unheard of.

Thanks so much for helping me raise my ACT that extra two points. My 33 put me one point above the scholarship's average. There were over 250 applicants this year for the scholarship, so I know that every point counted. Hope you enjoy the rest of your spring. I know my brother is looking forward to taking one of your classes soon!

-Nicole

How to deal with in-state residency rules?

This varies from state to state. I had a student (and his brother) who purchased an old house on the campus of his out-of-state college. This made them both in-state residents which meant they did not have to pay out-of-state tuition. However, I have been told Colorado restricts such maneuvers. I have had students "live" with relatives in order to avoid paying out-of-state tuition. Again, every state is different, so do your research and ask the colleges you are considering.

When is the best time to fill out FASFA?

Ferguson, author of **Crazy U**, has a section dedicated to FASFA. It will make you laugh and cry as it serves as another example of how the federal government needs to get out of our lives. There are no statistical formulas that use common sense to determine what a family can and cannot afford. In short, the formulas are arbitrarily designed by unelected bureaucrats. Assume you do not qualify for help. If you do qualify, assume there will be no funds for you due to the current recession and unstable economy that does not appear to be ending anytime soon.

> **WARNING:** Some schools may require family to complete FASFA prior to a scholarship package being offered. Ask each school what their FASFA policy is: required, recommended, neutral.

Our son is an Eagle Scout. How does that help him in this process?

One, there may be scholarships exclusively for Eagle Scouts, so I would encourage you to check on that with national, state, and local Boy Scout organizations. An Eagle Scout most likely has participated in events that were great learning experiences. Sharing those events with an admissions officer can help.

The above could apply to any organization whether it is local, state, national, or some combination of all three. Again, never be afraid to ask and don't assume they don't have such scholarships. You may be pleasantly surprised.

How do you match the college to my twins' abilities?

How did you match the high school your twins attend to their ability? The reality is that for most one's K-12 education has a greater impact on a person's life than the college education. Your twins' abilities may not even be fully developed or manifested at this time. A lot changes those first two years of college once students get out of high school. I see it every year. It's quite fascinating. Don't focus on trying to find a school to match your twins' abilities because you will stress yourself out. The better goal is to find a school they both like, that is cost effective, and one that will give great financial consideration if both attend the same university.

IMPORTANT: Having siblings attend the same school, especially twins, can really help with the emotional transition from high school to college. It's like taking part of your family to college with you.

What are strategies for students during their junior and senior years to build a strong college application if they are NOT in the top of their class rankings and do not have the highest ACT scores? How can they be competitive? What kind of activities, employment, etc. should they be involved in? (Jason's note: this student attends a very competitive public school.)

The senior year is important because too many students take the year off (senioritis) and then it catches up with them during the first semester of college. High school students need to maintain their focus that final year as it easy to get distracted because it is the "final" year. Students should definitely take a math class because most colleges require a math class and it's easier to do one during the first semester of college.

Students should try to include as many dual-credit classes as possible. Take advantage of those classes as they help lower the cost of college by eliminating the need to take them later. If dual-credit courses are not available or do not work in the student's schedule, then the student should consider AP classes. AP classes are intended to be more rigorous than traditional classes as they are intended to incorporate college-level intensity.

> **WARNING:** As stated earlier in the book, just because AP is in the course title does not necessarily mean it is an AP level course. Verify that the past performances have met the 80/80 standards.

Classes do not necessarily need to be taken during school hours. I've had many students take community college classes in the evenings, over the summer, and also online. If your high school does not offer AP classes and you would like to do one, then look for online AP classes and get permission to incorporate a study hall in your schedule where you can work on this class online.

What can a student do during their senior year to build a strong college application?

Colleges focus on the first three years of high school. They have to. College applications are submitted during the first few months of the senior year. Colleges cannot use the senior year because it is not complete. The reality is that most colleges make their acceptance decisions before the fall semester of the senior year is complete. This makes the junior year even more important.

A lot can happen during the junior year. Class ranks and grade point averages can change a lot. This happens at small and big schools, private and public. The student should make it a goal to get straight As during their junior year. This is the most important year in high school as the courses are a lot harder than the first two years of high school and colleges know it. I have had students who messed around their first two years of high school, got Bs, Cs, and some As, got all As or mostly As as juniors, and then when meeting with colleges they were honest about not working as hard as they should have when they began high school, but grew up and got serious during their junior year.

Colleges understand that some students are immature when they start high school. If the student can demonstrate that they have matured through high school and are ready for their challenges of college then an admissions officer may be willing to give the student a chance. Beware. The opposite is also true. If a student does well as a freshmen and sophomore but struggles dramatically as a junior, then that sends up red flags to an admissions officer.

Endnotes

[1] Mosbergen, Dominique. "Cost Of College Degree In U.S. Has Increased 1,120 Percent In 30 Years, Report Says." *The Huffington Post*. TheHuffingtonPost.com, 15 Aug. 2012. Web. 21 Nov. 2013.

[2] Snyder, Dr. Bonnie. "A Temporary Solution for Jobless College Grads." *The Huffington Post*. TheHuffingtonPost.com, 16 July 2012. Web. 23 Nov. 2013.

[3] CCAP. "Is America Saturated with College Grads?" *Forbes*. Forbes Magazine, 20 Dec. 2010. Web. 23 Nov. 2013.

[4] Rate, Economists Call That Figure the "mal-employment" "Recent College Grads Face 36% 'mal-employment' Rate." *CNNMoney*. Cable News Network, 25 June 2013. Web. 21 Nov. 2013.

[5] "29 Shocking Facts That Prove That College Education In America Is A Giant Money Making Scam." *INTELLIHUB*. N.p., n.d. Web. 23 Nov. 2013.

[6] "Starting Salaries of New College Graduates Drop 1.3% - USATODAY.com." Starting Salaries of New College Graduates Drop 1.3% - USATODAY.com. N.p., n.d. Web. 23 Nov. 2013.

[7] "Graduate from College; Live at Home? | Admit This!" *Graduate from College; Live at Home? | Admit This!* N.p., n.d. Web. 23 Nov. 2013. <http://www.collegeview.com/admit/?p=1553>.

[8] "Why Optimism Is Your Worst Investing Enemy." *MarketWatch*. N.p., n.d. Web. 23 Nov. 2013.

[9] "Stocks Rise; Dow Closes above 14,000." *The Christian Science Monitor*. The Christian Science Monitor, n.d. Web. 23 Nov. 2013.

[10] "Closing Milestones of the Dow Jones Industrial Average." *Wikipedia*. Wikimedia Foundation, 21 Nov. 2013. Web. 21 Nov. 2013.

[11] Fleetwood, Chad, and Kristina Shelley. "The Outlook for College Graduates, 1998 - 2008: A Balancing Act." *Occupational Outlook Quarterly* (2000): n. pg. 3-9 Web. 23 Nov. 2013.

[12] "Why It's a Terrible Time to Be a College Grad." *Chicago Grid*. N.p., n.d. Web. 23 Nov. 2013.

[13] Cummins, Denise, Dr. "Why Recent College Graduates Can't Find Jobs." *Psychology Today*. N.p., 11 Nov. 2013. Web. 23 Nov. 2013. <www.psychologytoday.com>.

[14] "Salary Survey: Average Starting Salary for Class of 2013 Grads Increases 2.4 Percent." *Salary Survey: Average Starting Salary for Class of 2013 Grads Increases 2.4 Percent*. N.p., n.d. Web. 24 Nov. 2013. <https://naceweb.org/s09042013/salary-survey-average-starting-class-2013.aspx>.

[15] "You Got College Credit for That?" *MNN*. N.p., n.d. Web. 26 Nov. 2013. <http://www.mnn.com/lifestyle/arts-culture/photos/15-bizarre-college-courses/you-got-college-credit-for-that>.

[16] "Advanced Placement." *U of I Admissions:*. N.p., 27 Nov. 2013. Web. 28 Feb. 2014. <http://admissions.illinois.edu/academics/placement_ap.html>.

[17] "UI Trustees Approve Tuition, More | News-Gazette.com." *LIVE: UI Trustees Approve Tuition, More | News-Gazette.com*. News-Gazette, 23 Jan. 2014. Web. 07 Feb. 2014. <http://www.news-gazette.com/news/local/2014-01-23/live-ui-trustees-approve-tuition-more.html>.

[18] "For News Media." *UCLA Sets New Undergraduate Applications Record / UCLA Newsroom*. N.p., n.d. Web. 26 Nov. 2013. <http://newsroom.ucla.edu/portal/ucla/ucla-sets-new-undergraduate-applications-242778.aspx>.

[19] "Undergraduate Full-Time Employment." *BCS: Business Career Services at the University of Illinois Urbana-Champaign*. N.p., n.d. Web. 26 Nov. 2013. <http://business.illinois.edu/bcs/recruiters/statistics/UG_stats.aspx>.

[20] "Intercollege Transfers." *College of Business: University of Illinois Urbana-Champaign*. N.p., n.d. Web. 26 Nov. 2013. <http://business.illinois.edu/undergrad/admissions/intercollege-transfers.aspx>.